What's Your Sign?

A Cosmic Guide for Young Astrologers

ISBN 0-448-42693-5   A B C D E F G H I J

What's Your Sign?

A Cosmic Guide for Young Astrologers

By Madalyn Aslan

Illustrated by Jennifer Kalis

Grosset & Dunlap · New York

DEAR FUTURE ASTROLOGER:

I started being an astrologer when I was seven years old. When I found out what it was all about, I thought it was the coolest thing. Astrology gave me access to a secret door inside myself. It helped me discover places I had known in myself all along, but had never found the words for. Even cooler, it also helped me figure out stuff about other people without them even *telling* me. It became my secret handshake.

Astrology can be your secret handshake, too. It's a way of telling details about someone without them actually telling *you*. It's your guide to unlocking the inner personalities of the people around you—your family, your friends, your teachers and classmates, even your secret crush! It's like learning a whole new language, one that is thousands and thousands of years old!

In fact, astrology is the world's *oldest* science. We've found star charts made by Egyptian astrologers in 4200 B.C.! And back in the old days, you even went to see your astrologer if you felt sick. Your diagnosis wasn't complete without a horoscope! The flu was called influenza because doctors said you got it under the *influence* of certain planets. So astrology has been with us for a long, long time.

It works like this: Everyone is born at a certain time, in a certain spot. Your birth is a burst of energy, which fuses with a surrounding force field. That force field is made up of the positions of the sun, the moon, and the planets at the *exact* moment of your birth. It's also made up of your normal everyday environment. All these things together mean that you are as physically linked to the solar system as anything you see around you.

We know that the solar system is around us; we live in it! The question is, how are we affected by it? For starters, we know that the Sun keeps every life-form on our Earth alive by giving us heat and light. These are easy enough to measure, right? Well, believe it our not, based on when and where we are born, the sun also gives each of us certain *character* traits. These traits are our Sun sign traits. We may not be able to measure them exactly, but we feel and express these character traits just as surely as we feel the sun's heat and light that we need to survive.

There's more to astrology than just the Sun signs, though. You have *ten* different planets in your astrological chart! And they all interact with each other in countless different ways to determine who you are.

But even just starting with the Sun signs is a pretty awesome place to start. Your Sun sign tells what you want in life, what you care about, who you get along with, and what you're good at. There are twelve Sun signs—Aries, Taurus, Gemini, Cancer, Leo, Virgo, Libra, Scorpio, Sagittarius, Capricorn, Aquarius, and Pisces—and each one displays specific personality traits.

It's fun to try to guess someone's sign once you've learned the traits of each one. Here is a quick spin around the zodiac:

Aries is bold, energetic, and daring.

Taurus is loyal, perceptive, and a problem solver.

Gemini is talkative, curious, and funny.

Cancer is feeling, self-protective, and family oriented.

Leo is confident, original, and a leader.

Virgo is hardworking, modest, and helpful.

Libra is charming, peace-loving, and a debater.

Scorpio is determined, loyal, and intuitive.

Sagittarius is fun, blunt, and adventurous.

Capricorn is persistent, disciplined, and supportive.

Aquarius is rebellious, creative, and passionate about the truth.

Pisces is sensitive, sympathetic, and a dreamer.

You're probably asking: how can the whole world be divided up into twelve types? Well, astrology doesn't say that *all* people born under the same sign are exactly alike. In fact, astrology says that everyone is totally *different*. That's because at the moment of any given person's birth into the world, there's a lineup of the sun, moon, and planets that will never be repeated because the whole universe is moving *every second*. That means that everyone has a completely different astrololgical chart, even twins. Astrology simply shows us that people born under a particular sign will *probably* display certain personality traits.

Knowing all this means you can put astrology to work for *you*. All it takes is looking and seeing. In fact, you form impressions of people all the time without even realizing you're doing it. You look at people and you take in their way of doing things and of relating to people, their likes and dislikes, even their sense of style, all to get a sense of who they are. Astrology just takes this one step further, giving us a language to talk about what we see and already know.

All it takes is practice. Start with your own sign. Learn your sign's traits and see how they apply to you. Then check out who else has your sign: family, friends, crushes, neighbors, even pets. Everyone is different, of course, but if you pay attention you'll start to notice some definite similarities. (Astrology is most fun when two people are the same sign, but seem completely different. That's when you become a supersleuth and dig deeper, beyond all those surface differences!)

Next, move on to the other Sun signs. Start writing down the signs of everyone you know and comparing their personalities to the profiles in this book. You'll start to figure out how it all works sooner than you think, because once you familiarize yourself with the signs' traits, you can guess almost anyone's sign. And after a while, you'll even be able to tell without double-checking. You'll become an observer of human behavior, and like noticing that someone is friendly or shy, you just pick it up. While everyone thinks you're a wizard with mysterious powers, the truth is you've studied astrology! *Only you will know!*

But don't get too cocky: you must always, always test yourself. When I read a book, I figure out the signs of the characters. I also figure out the signs of my favorite celebrities. The cool part is you can check out any celeb's sign really easily, especially on the web. Plus, a lot of hot celebs and their signs are listed at the end of each chapter in this book.

Like many astrology books, this guide talks about signs you might not necessarily get along with. Lots of astro books say things like "Virgo and Sagittarius don't mix," or "Aries and Libra clash." It's true to some extent that certain signs aren't usually the best matches, but that just means you have to try twice as hard to get along with someone totally opposite you. When you make the effort, you'll often discover that the friendship you make is twice as worth it! The most important thing is to stay curious, stay open, and just have some good old cosmic fun.

I hope this guide gives you that, and that it starts you off on a most excellent journey. Go for it!

All the very—stellar—best,

Madalyn Aslan,
wizard astrologer from the age of 7.

ARIES

ARIES

YOUR SPECIAL TIME: March 21–April 19

You were born at the beginning of all new life on Earth—spring. You are the pure energy of a flower bursting open and reaching to the Sun. March 21 is the first day of spring, and your sign is the first sign of the zodiac. See, you are first in everything!

YOUR AWESOME TRAITS

You're the explorer who takes risks, the life of the party who gets the dancing going. You're the first to talk, to dare, to think new ideas. You're bold, energetic, and daring. You're fast, fun, brave, independent, curious, adventurous, determined, bossy, loyal, generous, and lucky. The greatest playwright of all time, William Shakespeare, wrote about your star in his famous comedy *All's Well That Ends Well*.

Helena: Monsieur Parolles, you were born under a charitable star.
Parolles: Under Mars, I.
Helena: I especially think, under Mars.

Charitable means *kind*. Shakespeare was saying that your star is kind to you and gives you killer luck! Like Aries magician Harry Houdini, the famous daredevil whose tricks included being tied up underwater. He escaped every time!

OF ALL THE ANIMALS, YOU ARE MOST LIKE . . . A Ram

Rams like to leap into the air, crashing heads
and knocking horns. Have you ever heard
of a "battering ram"? They were used to
knock down enemy gates and doors.
Charging headfirst also helps you protect your
secret soft spot—which is not being liked.

WHO WAS YOUR ARIES RAM?

You've probably heard of Jason and the Golden Fleece. The Golden Fleece
came from the Aries ram. This golden ram was magical and famous in
ancient Greece. He was brave and rescued a young
prince who was in danger. The gods rewarded him with a
constellation in the Sky Star Walk of Fame. You
can see it in the night sky, reminding us how
brave you are and how you protect your
loved ones.

YOUR RULING PLANET: Macho Mars

Mars is the star of power, adrenalin, and drive. It is
the planet of movers and shakers. And man, does
Mars *rule*! It has the largest volcano in the
solar system (Olympus Mons), a mountain the
size of North America (Tharsis), and a canyon
over two thousand miles long. Mars glows
bright red in our sky and gives us its power from
millions of miles away! Its energy gives all of us
Earthdwellers guts and determination, but since Mars
is your special planet, you get an extra surge.

WHO WAS YOUR MARS?

Mars was the Roman god of war. The Greeks called him Ares, which is how we got the name Aries. Ares means "bright and burning one." Ares was the hero of every battle. Even on TV, the heroines in battle are played by *Aries*! Can you guess who? *Xena: Warrior Princess* (played by Aries Lucy Lawless) and *Buffy, the Vampire Slayer* (played by Aries Sarah Michelle Gellar).

THE PART OF YOUR BODY THAT ARIES RULES: Your Head

Aries bump their heads and get more migraines than any other sign. It's lucky they have hard heads, because curious Aries goes *ahead* and plunges in *head*first. You're hard*headed* and *head*strong. You like to be at the *head* of a race, and *head* of your class. Sometimes you even get a big *head*. Well, who wouldn't if they could do what you can?

IN YOUR ELEMENT: Fire

Aries is a fire sign. You have fiery opinions and heated arguments about what you believe. Watch your combustible temper!

YOUR LUCKY . . .

☆ **Colors:** Your lucky colors, like the color of your planet Mars, are red and maroon. In fact, Mars is called the Red Planet. And talk about fire . . . did you know that if you wear red or maroon you feel warmer? Try it!

☆ **Metal:** Iron. That's no surprise—the surface of your planet Mars is made up of iron oxide!

☆ **Precious stone:** Diamond. Diamond is the strongest valuable stone we know.

☆ **Day of the week:** The luckiest day of the week for Aries is Tuesday. Why? "Tuesday," in French, is *mardi*, which means "from Mars." So, schedule all the things you want to be lucky on Tuesdays

IN SCHOOL

Competition and challenge get you going. If there's a test, you'll learn what's important in ten seconds flat, and smile when you beat out your classmates for the top grade. You usually know the answers and aren't shy about talking in class. You're brilliant at sports and athletics, drama, inventing things, making up adventure stories, and leading clubs and discussions.

WITH YOUR TEACHERS

You get bored easily, so your fave teachers are the imaginative and funny ones who act out their classes and teach the lessons with stories. Unlike a Capricorn or Virgo, you're not interested in learning the rules of math or writing—you prefer to get it on your own. You're independent and don't like to follow orders. So for success, you'll need *lots* of self-discipline.

ON THE PLAYGROUND

While you're still a kid, you're like the Aries ram, leaping into the air and butting heads. Competitive sports are a great way for you to let off steam. Even when you're older, you'll still be the one inventing new games for you and your friends to play.

WITH YOUR FRIENDS

Aries have a lot of friends, and usually one or two best friends. You love to explore with your gang. You come up with new ideas for what to do, and you *have* to get outside. What hurts you most is when your friends don't support you.

WITH YOUR FAMILY

It's hard for Aries to sit still or be cooped up inside, so you're lucky if you have a family who mountain climbs (or hikes or does anything physical, as long as it's outside)! Otherwise, you probably argue with your brothers or sisters, even though you love them, and you can be quite a challenge to your parents, too. In spite of this, you're crazy about your family, and you love sharing holidays and birthdays the best.

TRUE LOVE

Aries are very romantic and daydream about their perfect hero or heroine. You become smitten instantly, but lose interest if your crush is a slowpoke or doesn't measure up. But when you set your heart on somebody—that's it!
Best Love Matches: Leo, Sagittarius, Aries, and Gemini. *Sometimes* your opposite sign, Libra.

WHICH SIGNS YOU GROOVE WITH; Which Signs You Don't

The easiest signs for you are the other fire signs. That's Leo, Sagittarius, and Aries (although you lock horns with fellow rams when mad). *You talk the same talk.* You might have to shout to be heard, but it's fun, isn't it? Capricorn's and Scorpio's constant planning makes you impatient, but you can deal. The hardest for you are choosy Virgo and sensitive Cancer. Try to remember that they feel as deeply as you do, they just express it in different ways. Virgo worries, and Cancer withdraws.

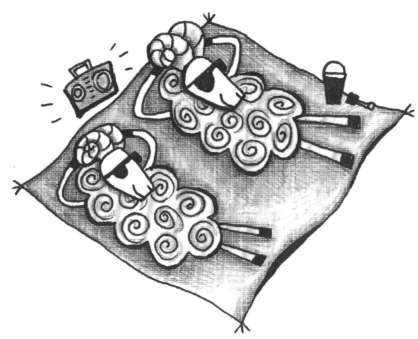

HOW TO SPOT AN ARIES

Look for the person who's taking over the conversation, school play, dance floor, football field, and probably your heart! You say you know an Aries who's shy and quiet? Check them out more. Are they director or head of anything? Do they do their own thing, in their own way? You'll surprise—and please—any Aries by guessing their sign. One of the nicest things in life is getting a ram's full attention.

OKAY, SO YOU'RE NOT AN ARIES . . .

⭐ **But Your Crush Is**

Your crush turns hot and cold, but don't worry, it's nothing to do with you. The love of your life is just off living his or her own Technicolor movie, absorbed in the everyday drama that always seems to follow Aries. And beware: Heroes have a lot of crushes, so you have to *tell* them you like them. Unlike the water signs, they can't read your secret signals. *Secret Tip*: Flattery and attention work!

⭐ **But Your Best Friend Is**

This one's a riot, and you *love* being his or her best friend. The only thing is, your best friend thinks he or she *owns* you! You do all the things that your BF wants to do, and your ace pal even makes you think it's all *your* idea! Plus, he or she might blame you if anything goes wrong. But no one else makes you laugh *so* much!

⭐ **But Your Brand-new Friend Is**

Be prepared for takeoff! With your new friend, you do all the things you've always dreamed of and never dared to actually *do*. You'll get in a ton of scrapes from this rough cutie, but it's worth it: An Aries makes you feel on top of the world. Just make sure you're supportive or you'll really hurt his or her feelings.

☆ But Your Teacher Is

This teacher has the best, most fun class, with the brightest kids. You were lucky to get into his or her class. Yeah, you know all that. But why does this cool teacher keep talking so much, then? And never give you time to answer the questions? And, of course, you're expected to get A's!

☆ But Your Parent Is

A parent who is an Aries will sword fight with you in the kitchen if you happen to be studying fencing at school. Your Aries mom or dad will make up new games, playact, and give you everything in the world for your birthday and on all the holidays. Your 'rent is very ambitious for you, and can push you in front of life's camera *way* young. He or she wants you to be best in everything.

☆ But Your Sister or Brother Is

Your Aries sibling barges into your room, tells you what to do, and cries if he or she doesn't get the best presents. You get so sick of your sibling, you could puke. But he or she will give you their last dollar, and will save your life when it counts.

☆ But Your Pet Is

Aries kitties are like Superman, leaping to impossible heights. They are even more daring and physical than the average cat—and Aries is never average, of course! Aries puppies never shut up. They grow to be slurpy and affectionate, and you just love them more than anyone.

ARIES ASTRO-JOTTER

ARIES STARLETS:
Claire Danes: April 12, 1979
Heath Ledge: April 4, 1979
Mandy Moore: April 10, 1984
Haley Joel Osment: April 10, 1988
Julia Stiles: March 28, 1981

ARIES HIGHEST HONORS
Leonardo da Vinci, artist and inventor: April 15, 1452
Secretariat, winning racehorse: March 30, 1970
Wilbur Wright, inventor of the airplane: April 16, 1867

FAVORITE ARIES CHARACTERS
Van Slanzer de Fanel (Escaflowne)
Lucy (Charlie Brown)

TAURUS

YOUR SPECIAL TIME: April 20–May 20

You are born when the land is most lush and green. Farmers plant their crops during Taurus. The Earth is strong, and the soil is ready to grow food. April 22 is Earth Day, when we celebrate the beauty of the Earth. *And* when we celebrate Taurus, a beautiful Earth sign!

YOUR AWESOME TRAITS

You are the sign of common sense, the bull's-eye that tells it like it is. You make the best friend in the world: You're loyal, affectionate, patient, dependable, strong, generous, gentle, and comforting. You overcome all obstacles and are a practical everyday miracle worker. You make the rest of us wonder how would we ever manage without you? You can do anything you set your mind to, from cranking out a *Hamlet* in three weeks, like genius Taurus William Shakespeare, or saving lives, like determined Taurus Florence Nightingale. Best of all, you never forget to just sit back and luxuriously smell the flowers, like quiet Ferdinand the Bull in the old story.

OF ALL THE ANIMALS, YOU'RE MOST LIKE . . . A Bull

A bull will graze quietly in a pasture, until it's disturbed—and then watch out! Its will, and especially its strength, are legendary. You can't make a bull do *anything* he doesn't want to do.

WHO WAS YOUR TAURUS BULL?

Taurus is one of the zodiac's oldest constellations. It was named between 4000 and 2000 B.C., when Egyptian farmers saw Taurus in the sky at the *exact* time the Nile River receded back far enough so that they could plow their fields. Thus, the bull became the sacred god of fertility, honored for providing food from the Earth. Today, the Audubon Society is committed to preserving the Earth, and guess who started *that*? Yup, John James Audubon, a Taurus!

YOUR RULING PLANET: Sweet Venus

Sweet Venus is called Earth's "sister." No other planet comes as close to us in orbit, or is so like Earth in size, mass, and density. But Venus has the highest temperatures in the solar system after the Sun—around 900 degrees Fahrenheit! It is an example of what could happen to the Earth if we do not take care of it. Taurus, more than any other sign, knows about the care and the cost of things, and it is Venus's energy that gives Taurus the will to maintain a sweet and beautiful life.

WHO WAS YOUR VENUS?

Venus—or Aphrodite as she is sometimes called—was the goddess of love and beauty. The name Aphrodite means "born from sea foam." Do you know the beautiful painting by the famous painter Botticelli of the woman standing in a huge seashell? That is Aphrodite! Her purpose was to help us enjoy our five senses. This is especially true for Taurus, as you're a practical, earthy sign: You trust what you see, touch, taste, hear, or smell.

THE PART OF YOUR BODY THAT TAURUS RULES:
Your Throat and Neck

Taurus gets more sore throats and laryngitis than any
other sign, which is funny since so many of the world's
best singing voices belong to Tauruses! Barbra Streisand,
Stevie Wonder, Cher, Enya, Billy Joel, Janet Jackson,
Enrique Iglesias—they're all Tauruses!

IN YOUR ELEMENT: Earth

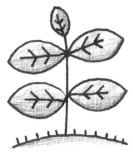

Taurus is an Earth sign. You are down to earth, and
people often comment that you have your feet on the
ground. But sometimes it is like your feet are *planted*
on that ground! You hate being moved from *your*
ground and you hate change in *your* routine. *Terra* is
Latin, meaning "earth." This is where we get the word
"territorial"—a perfect description for Taurus!

"I don't like it when things change—like even the time!"
—LYLA, *Taurus*

YOUR LUCKY . . .

☆ **Color:** Your lucky colors are green and baby blue, the
colors of the earth and the sky. You love nature and you
like to feel calm and comfortable. Wearing these colors has
the most soothing, gentle effect on your state of mind. Check
them out!

☆ **Metal:** Copper

☆ **Precious Stone:** Emerald

☆ **Day of the week:** The luckiest day of the week for Taurus is Friday. Why? "Friday," in French, is *vendredi*. The word *vendredi* comes from sweet Venus, *your* ruling planet. So, schedule the things you want to go extra sweetly for you on Fridays!

IN SCHOOL

You have steady concentration, and once you learn something you never forget it. You're not a show-off like your Aries and Leo classmates, and you don't talk all the time like a Gemini, but you shine in tests because you prepare so well. You excel in music, painting, and anything to do with science and the Earth.

WITH YOUR TEACHERS

You tend to be the teacher's pet because you work hard and don't act up in class. Teachers also like you to lead the group because of your responsibility, maturity, common sense, good judgment, and love of fair play. However, you can sometimes unnerve your teachers: You *insist* on the visible truth and you speak up quickly when they get their facts wrong!

ON THE PLAYGROUND

You're strong, healthy, and athletic, with lots of stamina to boot: You keep going in games *long* after your classmates quit. You like being with a group, but you're also just as happy to be left alone to your own devices. And if someone pushes you too much, you dig your feet into the ground, just like the bull that you are, and charge!

WITH YOUR FRIENDS

Your friends are number one in your book, and you give them so much, they wish there were a million of you! They count on you, and like knowing that you're there for them. Sometimes, though, you can be a little gullible, and there's no greater hurt for you than being lied to or betrayed by a friend.

WITH YOUR FAMILY

You love a comfy home, yummy meals, family rituals, and all the things that involve your fave routines. If your parents want you to do something, only practical explanations *or* affection will win you over—never them yelling orders at you. You fight with your brothers or sisters if they take your things or intrude on your space. (It's that terra, territorial thing!)

TRUE LOVE

Looks can be important to you, but because you're a Taurus—an Earth sign—you want the *real thing.* You want someone who's there for you and who won't take advantage of your generosity.
Best Love Matches: Taurus, Virgo, Capricorn, and Cancer

WHICH SIGNS YOU GROOVE WITH; Which Signs You Don't

The easiest signs for you are the other Earth signs: Taurus, Virgo, and Capricorn. You guys all love the same things, like nature hikes, practical jokes, and comfy clothes. Libra makes your next best friend, because this sign has your same ruling planet, Sweet Venus. (You both *love* chocolate!) Gemini's changes can drive you nuts, and Leo can sometimes get too bossy, but you can deal. The hardest signs for you are airy Aquarius and goof-off Sagittarius. Sometimes it seems like the only thing you can count on with *these* two is a fun time—so just enjoy them!

HOW TO SPOT A TAURUS

When they're relaxing, look for stillness and deliberation in the way they move. But then, when they're running around like maniacs, listen to their footsteps. Tauruses land heavily, plonking on the ground like bulls' hooves.

Even if they're graceful dancers (like Taurus Fred
Astaire) they stamp on the floor for rhythm.
Taurus eyes are limpid and
steady. They don't dart around
or look away. And if you ask
them a question, they will
answer you using practical,
solid points. (The great Taurus
philosopher Socrates is a famous
example of the bull's super-logical question-and-answer form.) Finally, you
can always spot Tauruses by the way they eat. Food is a *god* to them, and
they chew thoroughly, tasting every single bite.

Okay, So You're Not a Taurus . . .

☆ **But Your Crush Is**

Tauruses are pretty traditional: The girls like manly boys, and the boys like girly girls. They like to take their own sweet time before making a move. And the way to their hearts is definitely through their stomachs!

Secret Tip: More than anything, bulls like feeling comfortable. If they feel uneasy, they withdraw.

☆ **But Your Best Friend Is**

Taurus makes a really good best friend, but be warned: Taurus likes the truth, plain and simple.

Your best friend doesn't like to play games and will be your best friend forever as long as you stick to the truth and never lie to him or her.

☆ **But Your Brand-new Friend Is**

This new friend gives you practical advice about what works for you and shows you how to take care of yourself. Especially when you're shopping at the mall. Tauruses *love* to buy things!

☆ **But Your Teacher Is**

Your Taurus teacher is really nice, and is always ready to help you. He or she explains everything slowly and thoroughly, then waits for everyone to write it down, word for word. At the end of class you feel calm because you know you'll remember what your teacher has said when you take the test.

☆ But Your Parent Is

Your Taurus parent makes sure you enjoy the best of everything: the best meals, the best TV nights, and even the best (that is, the *most*!) money for buying you new clothes. It's great—your 'rent even gives you an allowance earlier than some of the other kids! You love all the attention, but it can get a little dull, that's all. Sometimes, you can't wait to go to college.

☆ But Your Sister or Brother Is

A brother or sister who's a Taurus can be pretty spoiled. Taurus sibs just hold on to Mom if you criticize them. They're pretty cute, too. They love sweets, and you can make them do almost anything if you bribe them with chocolate.

☆ But Your Pet Is

Taurus cats are the best cats of all, because Taurus rules cats. See how they just like to be comfortable? And loved? They just want to be with you forever. They hate if you move them or change anything around, and they're always going round sniffing to establish their territory again. Your Taurus dog is the same, but a little louder and rougher.

TAURUS ASTRO-JOTTER

TAURUS STARLETS

Jessica Alba: April 28, 1981

Lance Bass: May 4, 1979

Jason Biggs: May 12, 1978

Kirsten Dunst: April 30, 1982

Jamie-Lynn Sigler: May 15, 1981

TAURUS HIGHEST HONORS

Willie Mays, baseball player: May 6, 1931

William Shakespeare, playwright and poet: April 23, 1564

Malcolm X, civil rights leader: May 19, 1925

FAVORITE TAURUS CHARACTERS

Nancy Drew

Eeyore (Winnie the Pooh)

Homer Simpson (*The Simpsons*)

GEMINI

YOUR SPECIAL TIME: May 21–June 20

The ancients gave the moons of this time very playful names. If you're a May Gemini, then you were born under the Milk Moon, Planting Moon, or Hare Moon. If you're a June Gemini, you were born under the Rose, Flower, Strawberry, or Mead Moon. Despite the names, your special time has nothing to do crops or work—so all Gemini has to do is *play* under all those Moons!

YOUR AWESOME TRAITS

You're smart, fun, charming, and friendly and full of energy, ideas, and fast talk. You're curious, original, adaptable, and funny. So funny! More comedians are born under Gemini than any other sign, like Dana Carvey, Jim Belushi, Gene Wilder, Dean Martin, Bob Hope, Stan Laurel, Tim Allen, and John Goodman. You can be a *little* bit nervous and you never sit still. You're the Peter Pan of the zodiac! You think a lot, but you're very verbal, and love wordplays. In fact, you're *extremely* clever with words. Do you know these? Quicksilver. Mercurial. Amusing. Witty. They all describe *you*!

OF ALL THE ANIMALS, YOU'RE MOST LIKE . . .
A Pair of Twin Monkeys

Just like clever, playful monkeys, you are fun to watch and always entertaining. (Being a Gemini—a "twin"—means you have *two* distinct sides, so

you are like two monkeys, not just one. That means twice the fun!) Monkeys play with and mimic the world around them. They are smart, responsive, and affectionate, descriptions that fit Gemini to a T. Not surprisingly, U.S. Census Bureau records show that more twins are born during the time of Gemini than at any other time of the year!

WHO WAS YOUR GEMINI?

In ancient Greece, two sets of twins were born. One pair was mortal, and one pair was immortal. Their mother, Leda, disguised as a beautiful swan, laid two eggs, one for each pair. The immortal twins were Pollux, a boy, and Helen, a girl. The mortal twins were Castor, a boy, and Clytemnestra, a girl. Legend has it that Jupiter, king of the gods, transformed Castor and Pollux (the boy twins of each pair) into the constellation Gemini, or The Twins. Thus, just like Gemini, you have two sides: an extraordinary (immortal) side, and an ordinary (mortal) side.

YOUR RULING PLANET: Instant-Messaging Mercury

Mercury is the star of thought. He is the fast-paced messenger planet. You know how fast you think? Well, Mercury orbits the Sun faster than any other planet in the solar system. It races round the Sun at 29.8 miles per second! Mercury's tiny, but it's got a huge job to perform. Its job is to deliver energy to the Earth by way of instant messages to the brain. It rules computers, technology, and all fast-thinking things. It was named after a famous messenger because it appears and disappears so fast, astronomers only see it a few times a year!

WHO WAS YOUR MERCURY?

Mercury was the Roman messenger of the gods, also known as Hermes in Greek. As the winged messenger,

he flew faster than the speed of light to deliver messages from one god to another, and between the heavens and humans.

THE PART OF YOUR BODY THAT GEMINI RULES:
Your Hands, Arms, Shoulders, and Lungs

Because your symbol is twins, you rule all the parts of the body that come in pairs: two arms, two hands, two lungs, two shoulders! You communicate a lot with your hands, arms, shoulders, and even lungs (you love to talk!). You also love wearing bracelets, bangles, and rings. You need to watch out for bronchitis and allergies (lung problems), and be careful of accidents with your hands, shoulders, and arms.

IN YOUR ELEMENT: Air

Gemini is an air sign, and since air rules thought and *you* are a figurative twin, you often think more than one thought at once. The word "air"  comes from the Latin *aer*. You have a super-gymnast brain, and for you, *aery* means fairy-quick thinking that's crazy-fast, exactly the way mischievous fairies move and flit about.

YOUR LUCKY . . .

☆ **Colors:** Your lucky colors are yellow and orange, the colors of energy and cheerfulness.

☆ **Metal:** Mercury. Mercury is used in thermometers to measure your temperature.

☆ **Precious Stone:** Agate. It's multicolored (multiple again—like twins!), and only semi-precious, which is good, since Gemini tends to lose and forget things!

☆ **Day of the week:** Wednesday. *Mercredi* is French for "Wednesday," and comes from Mercury, your ruling planet. So, schedule all the things you want to be lucky on Wednesdays.

IN SCHOOL

You have a mind that's inquisitive, mercurial (meaning quick—and quick-changing!), and you're an excellent writer. You talk nonstop, and you're often the class comic. You're very smart, and even if you only study right before a test, you still ace it. It's the long-term projects that are more of a challenge for you.

WITH YOUR TEACHERS

They love your quick mind and humor, and that you'll answer questions nobody else will. But they tell you to focus more on *finishing* things. You're always ready to move on to the next subject!

ON THE PLAYGROUND

You go from one group to another, always in search of something new and interesting. You flit around like a butterfly, first landing on one flower, then another. (Then maybe a tree! Just for a change . . .)

WITH YOUR FRIENDS

You're the wonderful friend who lifts people out of their ruts. You have tons of friends of all types and, true to your dual nature, you can sometimes seem like a split personality because you act differently with all your different pals. You always make friends with the new kids in school.

WITH YOUR FAMILY

More than any other sign, you think your family's cool, even if you're mad at them. You love it best when they take you traveling! If you feel they're not paying enough attention to you, you say smart and funny things to make them laugh.

TRUE LOVE

One side of you just wants to have fun and explore, be totally uncommitted; the other side of you wants a perfect, secure dream love. If you often seem to find something wrong with the very person you like the most, it's usually because you're hesitant about falling in love.

Best Love Matches: Aquarius, Libra, Gemini, and Aries

WHICH SIGNS YOU GROOVE WITH; Which Signs You Don't

The easiest signs for you to get along with are the other air signs: Aquarius, Libra, and Gemini. (With another Gemini, you can talk forever!) Aries, Sagittarius, and Leo make your next best friends because they're into adventure just like you, and also Pisces because they're so unusual. Taurus can be kind of boring for you, but you can deal. The hardest for you are Capricorn and Cancer. They want to *plan* everything! You prefer to be spontaneous!

HOW TO SPOT A GEMINI

See that person over there, talking fast, tilting his head like a bird, using his hands to communicate? If someone seems to have a nervous energy, you can safely say you've spotted a Gemini. Ask them! They love to talk! But you might also spot them in their staring-off-into-space mode, not talking at all. If you look closer, you will see they *are* talking—with *themselves*. Five different thoughts can run through their heads at once—they have to sort them *out somehow*! Geminis are also always moving, or going somewhere. In fact, statistics show that Geminis use public transportation more than any other sign. They tend to bump into people they know along the way, so they are usually late for things. Don't try to pin them down. They're vague about certain details. Like what they did yesterday. Finally, they love new information.

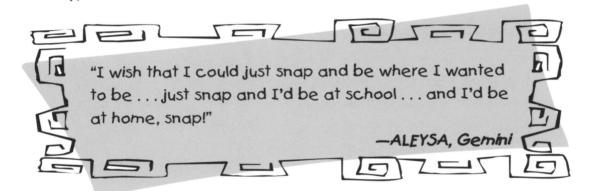

"I wish that I could just snap and be where I wanted to be . . . just snap and I'd be at school . . . and I'd be at home, snap!"

—ALEYSA, Gemini

☆ But Your Crush Is

Your crush grabs your attention right away. He or she is the one always making jokes and sounding really clever. If you want to laugh and have fun, Geminis are the perfect mates. But you have to be flexible. They can change their minds like *that*!

☆ But Your Best Friend Is

Is this the one giving you advice all the time? Jumping from topic to topic? Your best friend can change a lot and drive you crazy, but one thing's for sure: He or she is so much fun to be with!

☆ But Your Brand-new Friend Is

What a blast! It is way cool hanging out with a Gemini, and you don't want it to ever stop! This is the most entertaining friend you've had in a *long* time.

☆ But Your Teacher Is

You wish this teacher could teach *all* your classes, because he or she makes learning so much fun! Teachers who are Geminis are very smart, and have a lot of interesting theories. They give different sides of every question and answer. They also challenge you, ask you lots of difficult questions, and make you think hard.

☆ But Your Parent Is

Does your parent, like, always change the subject, or sometimes stop talking completely and stare into space? You like the way they hum or sing, and make jokes.

Gemini parents are what you call *educational* parents. They want you to be smart and curious. They also like to travel, so encourage them to take you along!

☆ But Your Sister or Brother Is

Your Gemini brother or sister is really competitive. It's not like your sib wants more attention from the 'rents. He or she just has to *compete*! It'll bug you less if you try to see it from your sibling's point of view. You're like a greyhound racing next to them—it just keeps them from being bored.

☆ But Your Pet Is

Gemini pets act like clowns, cat *or* dog. They wear funny expressions on their faces, and are always opening their eyes wide at everything. They're fun, but don't leave them alone too long—you don't want to see how they'll deal with getting bored! It's kind of like having *wild* pets.

GEMINI ASTRO-JOTTER

GEMINI STARLETS

Larisa Oleynik: June 7, 1981

TWINS Mary-Kate and Ashley Olsen: June 13, 1987

Natalie Portman: June 9, 1981

Leelee Sobieski: June 10, 1982

Venus Williams: June 17, 1980

GEMINI HIGHEST HONORS

Jacques Cousteau, deep-sea explorer: June 11, 1910

Miles Davis, jazz musician: May 26, 1926

Anne Frank, teenage diarist: June 12, 1929

FAVORITE GEMINI CHARACTERS

Bugs Bunny

Sherlock Holmes

Superman *and* his "alter ego" Clark Kent

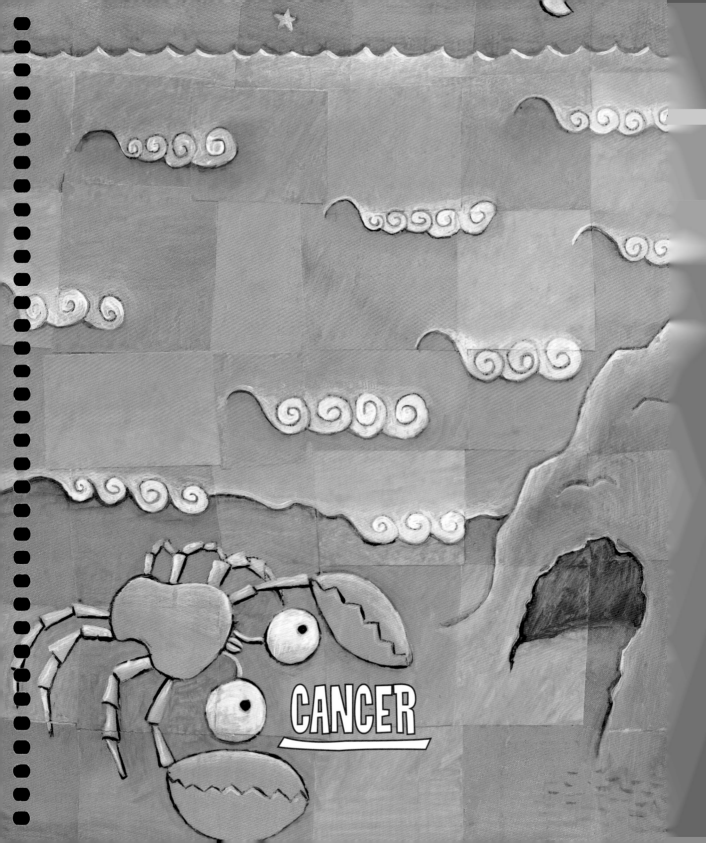

CANCER

YOUR SPECIAL TIME: June 21–July 22

June 21 begins the summer solstice and is the longest day of the year. You, sweet Crab, wish for good things to last forever. Solstice means "sun stands still." From this day, the days get shorter. This encourages you to hold on, like a crab, longer and longer.

YOUR AWESOME TRAITS

You are a tender heart on the inside, funny and flip on the outside. Next to Gemini, there are more comedians born in your sign than in any other. Look at the Famous Lunar Laugh List! Mike Meyers, Dan Aykroyd, Robin Williams, Bill Cosby, Mel Brooks, Freddie Prinz, Jr., and David Spade are all Cancer Crabs just to name a few. You are family-oriented, loveable, sensitive, imaginative, kind, loyal, and intuitive to a psychic degree! You are deep-feeling and forever persevering. You have a sharp and shrewd mind and you remember everything. You are protective of your friends and great at giving them advice. The most famous advice-givers are Crabs, from Dear Abby to the Dalai Lama. But take note: The Crab can go two ways. The shell or the heart? Kindness or crabbiness? It's your choice, Cancer.

OF ALL THE ANIMALS, YOU'RE MOST LIKE . . . A Crab

The crab is over 500 million years old. It has survived so long because it's smart and protects itself. Its home is its very body! Its shell is hard and protective, but inside its shell-home, the crab is soft and vulnerable. It has curious pop-out eyes that look up, watching out for seagulls and feet and other sea creatures. Like Chicken Little, worried about what's coming down!

WHO WAS YOUR CANCER?

In Egypt, your constellation was called the Stars of the Water, and it was of two turtles. The scarab beetle became Cancer's second symbol. Then, thousands of years later, the Greeks changed the scarab to a crab. And here you are. The turtle, the crab, and the scarab beetle all have a shell. It protects a sacred interior.

YOUR RULING PLANET: Magical Mystery Moon

The moon is the star of feelings, intuition, and memory. She is your emotional anchor planet. She moves the oceans and us, too, since 90 percent of our bodies are made up of water! Think about it. Inside every human and animal, 90 percent of who we are—especially our emotions and our unconscious—is being rhythmically moved like the tides. We can't see this gravitational force, but we can still feel it from 239,000 miles away. Sometimes, what is most powerful is invisible. You, lunar Cancer, already instinctively know this. (Luna means "moon" in Latin!)

WHO WAS YOUR MOON?

The Moon has always been related to the Mother. There are more births at the Full Moon and the New Moon than at any other time! Moon Goddess worship was the dominant religion throughout the world until 1500 B.C. She had many names. Diana, Hecate, and Artemis were just a few, and each had a different story. Even today many cultures, from Native American to Orthodox Jewish, base their  year on lunar months, not solar months. Interestingly, it is the last Sunday in June when most couples get married—this is during Cancer, which is Moon-Birth-Time!

THE PART OF YOUR BODY THAT CANCER RULES:
Your Stomach and Breasts

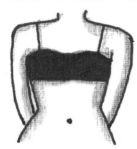 Your stomach and breasts get fuller or smaller depending on the fullness of the Moon, which is your ruling planet. For both girls and boys, breasts are a symbol of mothering. The stomach is where feelings are stored, and Cancer is very sensitive. So Crabs can frequently have stomach problems, even ulcers.

IN YOUR ELEMENT: Water

Water rules everything we're born with—instincts, intuition, feeling, and unconscious. Cancer is keeper of the ocean floor, where all life began. You know everything, psychically, just by feeling! And wouldn't you say your moods go back and forth like the tides?

YOUR LUCKY . . .

☆ **Colors:** Your lucky colors are sea green and silver, the colors of your powerful ocean home and the moon.

☆ **Metal:** Silver. Like glinting moonlight!

☆ **Precious stone:** Pearl. Pearls come from the inside of an oyster, inside a shell, deep from the sea.

☆ **Day of the week:** Monday. Mon-day is MOON-day. "Monday," in French, is lundi (which comes from lunar, luna meaning "moon" in Latin). So, schedule all the things you want to be lucky on Mondays.

IN SCHOOL

Even though you're a daydreamer, you are one of the hardest-working signs. Your mind becomes a photocopy of all that you see and hear. You love fairy tales, but if you want to be an accountant, go for it. You're better at counting money than anyone.

WITH YOUR TEACHERS

Your history teacher loves you. You remember dates better than anyone. You also tell great stories and jokes, which makes you a great writer or performer.

ON THE PLAYGROUND

You might appear to be a follower, but you're not. You are a born leader, you just don't shout it out. You're off quietly doing your own thing, or organizing everyone else's.

WITH YOUR FRIENDS

You're the zodiac mom, telling your friends how to take care of themselves and whom *not* to go out with. You're loyal and funny and protective. Sometimes you just need to be alone, to go inside your crab shell. You need solitude to balance your fun.

WITH YOUR FAMILY

Such a homebody! Sometimes it's like pulling teeth to get you outside. Especially away from your mom. (Did you know that baby crabs incubate for a whole year?) You love being inside your shell-home with your family. You save photos of every member of your family and you have whole collections stored in your room.

"I just love my family, and I just think they're the greatest. I like to be with them when we're doing small and insignificant things, like at home. I like to be in the home environment, just being together."
—ELIZABETH, Cancer

TRUE LOVE

You want true love so much, it hurts. And you don't even let anyone know! It's hard being you sometimes. Sometimes you feel so cut off from the rest of the world, you ache. Don't worry, Crabby. That hard shell you carry around is just protection, it doesn't have to cut you off from anything. *Secret Tip:* Your shell protects you all the time, so relax!

Best Love Matches: Scorpio, Pisces, Cancer, and Taurus

WHICH SIGNS YOU GROOVE WITH; Which Signs You Don't

The easiest signs for you are other water signs. You guys understand what the other is feeling, sometimes without even having to talk. Being with other Crabs is awesome: It's like you have a psychic bond, but you have to watch out for one another's ups and downs. Pisces is your soul-twin of the sea, and makes you laugh as much as Gemini. You guys make each other feel confident. Aries is way too harsh for the sensitive crab, and Aquarius is too out-there. Crabs need stability. Taurus can give you that.

HOW TO SPOT A CANCER

Because Cancerians are so connected to the Moon, look for the Moon—literally! Cancerian people often have round, moon-shaped faces. The Moon is all about feeling, and their faces show every-thing they have inside of them. Even though they are cute and funny and romantic, Cancers always have their eye on the future. They are dramatic about  being hurt and sometimes feel the world is against them. But how do you think they have survived for 500 million years? They focus on what's around them and never let go of what they want. Like a real crab, they hang on with their claws until one is broken—then they grow a new claw and hang on more! In spite of their sensitivity, they're smart tough cookies.

☆ But Your Crush Is

Watch how real-live crabs walk. It's never in a straight line. They're shy, so they go sideways, never straight. They circle you for a while before coming to rest in front of you. That's Cancer. So if you don't have a lot of patience, go somewhere else. *Secret Tip:* He or she won't say so, but your crush *loves* gentle, romantic gestures. And Cancers can wound easily, so play nice.

☆ But Your Best Friend Is

Cancer best friends are sympathetic and funny. They give you surprise gifts. They will always be your friend, unless you do something that really hurts them. They can be moody, and remember all their wounds way too much. The flip side is their humor (hysterical!) and the way they fuss over you, which is cozy.

☆ But Your Brand-new Friend Is

Your new Cancerian friend isn't really into venturing to new and different places, except through make-believe! Did you meet him or her online? Cancers love to live in their computers, and they make friends easily online. Even still, they take a while opening up—*while* being cutesy and funny.

☆ But Your Teacher Is

You feel you can trust this teacher, and this is the one you go to if you're having a problem. Cancerian teachers will *always* listen to what you have to say.

☆ But Your Parent Is

A Cancer parent is overprotective and very loving. You love the meals, the stories, and the bedtime rituals, but sometimes you just wanna say, loosen up, willya? Luckily, your Cancerian mom or dad is imaginative and great with stories, so if you want to give this parent a message, start there.

☆ But Your Sister or Brother Is

So secretive! What's that about? Your sibling is always squirreling away things in their room and he or she has a big PRIVATE sign on the bedroom door. Cancerian sibs remember every mean thing you say to them, but they're always the ones you go to when you need a good friend.

☆ But Your Pet Is

A Crabby dog will either be mopey, or spinning around with shining eyes. If you have a Crabby cat, the puffy feline sleeps all the time. Cancer animals have the same moods as Cancer humans, so be prepared for your pet's personality changes. Be *gentle*.

CANCER ASTRO-JOTTER

CANCER STARLETS
Topher Grace: July 12, 1978
Josh Hartnett: July 21, 1978
Michelle Kwan: July 7, 1980
Prince William: June 21, 1982
Jessica Simpson: July 10, 1980

CANCER HIGHEST HONORS
Helen Keller, blind, deaf, and mute educator: June 27, 1880
Nelson Mandela, South African leader and former president: July 18, 1918
The United States of America: July 4, 1776

FAVORITE CANCER CHARACTERS
Ken (Barbie's guy)
Linus (Charlie Brown)
LiSyaoran (*Sailor Moon*)

LEO

LEO

YOUR SPECIAL TIME: July 23–August 22

In Leo season, the Sun is at its most powerful. During this time the crops have been planted but won't be harvested until the sign of Virgo, in September. So all you need to do is enjoy yourself in anticipation of a great harvest! Looking forward to a shining future is what sunny, upbeat Leo is all about.

YOUR AWESOME TRAITS

The world wouldn't be any fun without Leos. You're a star! You're confident, generous, enthusiastic, powerful, warm, and expansive. You're also creative, brimming with ideas, charismatic, fun, loyal, sensitive, and a natural-born leader. You always get attention at parties. You're a fabulous dancer and a gorgeous show-off, and you make everyone feel good. And when the real crisis comes, just like the Cowardly Lion who protected Dorothy, you have your courage. You take care of those you love, and all *nice* people. You are intense about injustice. You will not be dissed, and if your family or friends are, you will roar to protect them. All Lions possess a kingdom, whether it's your home, circle of friends, or school. You are, without question, ruler of your pride. You are brilliant, and have so many gifts that you can choose the kind of life you want.

OF ALL THE ANIMALS, YOU ARE MOST LIKE . . . A Lion

 The Lion is King of the Beasts! Lions are royal, brave, luxurious, noble, and beautiful. They were made to be worshiped. And, like you, they occasionally roar to show their pride and strength.

WHO WAS YOUR LEO?

The constellation of Leo commemorates the magnificent Nemean lion. He roamed all over ancient Greece, slaying everyone who dared cross his path. The first of Hercules's Twelve Labors was to kill this almighty Nemean lion, but since the lion could not be hurt by mortal weapons, Hercules's arrows just bounced off his pelt. In the end, Hercules could win only by using his bare hands. He wore the lion's skin for the rest of his life, which helped him win his battles. This is what made him strong, and how he became the famous Hercules. The gods so admired the lion, they honored him with his own constellation in the Sky Star Walk of Fame.

YOUR RULING PLANET: Biggie Bombdiggety Sun

The Sun is the star of life, light, creativity, and joy. He is your life-force *god* planet. Using only *half a billionth* of its energy, this almighty star keeps every single life-form on Earth alive. The Sun is over a million times the size of our Earth. It burns 27 million degrees Fahrenheit and even from 93.2 million miles away we feel its life-giving power. Without our protective ozone layer, it could destroy us in a second. The Sun is bigger than all the other bodies in our solar system *combined.* It gives life, light, warmth, happiness! And guess who gets extra helpings? You!

WHO WAS YOUR SUN?

One of the Seven Wonders of the World is the Colossus of Rhodes, which is a one hundred-foot-tall bronze statue of Helios. Helios, also known as Apollo, was the sun god of light and truth. Helios found the best city on Earth, Delphi, to build a shrine for humankind to worship him. But Python, the huge serpent, was holding the city hostage. Helios won the city back, and put a prophetess in charge of his new shrine. No one can defeat the Sun!

THE PART OF YOUR BODY THAT LEO RULES:
Your Heart, Back, and Spine

The heart and spine are the center of us. They enable us to love and walk tall! Leos need to watch out for emotional strain and overexertion. They need *cat* naps. But most of all, they need to keep their hearts happy.

IN YOUR ELEMENT: Fire

Leo is a fire sign, and enjoys the pure light, passion, and inspiration of fire. But Leo fire is less combative than Aries fire. Cats always prefer the warmth and luxury of the hearth over battle!

YOUR LUCKY . . .

☆ **Colors:** Your lucky colors are gold and orange, the charismatic colors of the Sun.

☆ **Metal:** Gold. Pure gold. What else could it be?

☆ **Precious stone:** Ruby. Bloodred for life-force.

☆ **Day of the week:** SUN-DAY, because the sun is your ruling star. This is an honored day of worship and rest in many societies. So schedule all the things you want to be lucky on Sundays.

IN SCHOOL

The arts are a natural for you (there are more Leos in movies than any other sign, except Pisces). You're a born leader and organizer, and you inspire your classmates in discussion. You expect the best of yourself, and when you work hard, the sky's the limit.

WITH YOUR TEACHERS

They may pick you to be substitute teacher when they're out of the room, because they know you can handle it. Try not to charm them into giving you good grades. You know it's better for you in the long run if you earn them. Plus, you need *genuine* recognition of your greatness; you like knowing the kudos you receive are well-deserved.

ON THE PLAYGROUND

Who's the hottest of them all? Buzzed-about Leos have the most copycats of their style. Look at Madonna, Jennifer Lopez, and Howie Dorough! They are all lions. You start trends that *rock*.

WITH YOUR FRIENDS

You would give the world to your friends—and you do. Your friendship is golden. You're the most fun, have all the best ideas, and give  great advice. It is no coincidence that in the hit series *Friends*, half of the fab cast are Leos: Matt LeBlanc, Lisa Kudrow, and Matthew Perry!

WITH YOUR FAMILY

You love your family, but you want your freedom, too! Sometimes they want you to give up more than you like. But inviting friends back to your family castle is a blast.

TRUE LOVE

You live for love. You want someone you can look up to, someone who inspires you. You're willing to take a risk for the best. You need a royal mate who adores and worships you. Which is why Leos often end up marrying each other! **Best Love Matches:** Leo, Aries, Sagittarius, Libra, and Gemini

WHICH SIGNS YOU GROOVE WITH; Which Signs You Don't

The easiest signs are other fire signs because you all walk the same line of fire! Libra and Gemini make your next best friends. Taurus isn't exciting enough for you, and Scorpio can be a tad too controlling, but you can deal. The hardest for you are Pisces and Virgo. You'll want to be especially gracious and generous with these two signs precisely because you don't always understand them. And a royal lion's never caught unaware, right?

HOW TO SPOT A LEO

Inside every Leo is a star who believes in him or herself, even if they're quiet as a mouse. Just look for the brightest light in any gathering. Leos literally look like lions. They have manes of hair, often swept back, and an "I'm-being-adored" expression. They blink slowly, with heavy cat-lidded eyes. They move like cats, too: light on their feet, but with an intensity and a stateliness. Another give-away is that they often yawn when they're talking to someone. It's not rudeness. They're just acting like luxurious lions! From Bill Clinton to

Martha Stewart to Fidel Castro, the public either loves or hates them. Lions stay in the news. Mick Jagger, Madonna, Jackie O, Andy Warhol, Arnold Schwarzenegger, Coco Chanel, and Robert De Niro have all created trends that influenced whole generations. The World Wide Web is a Leo, born August 5, 1990, in Switzerland. MTV was also born under the sign of Leo, in 1981. Think of the world now without them. We can't!

"I'm quiet, but people notice me. A lot of kids say I'm stuck up, but that's not true!"

—GEOFFREY, Leo

Okay, So You're Not a Leo . . .

☆ But Your Crush Is

Leos love the dating ritual. But after the chase, if your crush decides you're the one, expect to be adored. *Secret Tip:* Leo guys don't like girls with lots of makeup. And Leo girls don't like cheap dates!

☆ But Your Best Friend Is

Leo best friends are unbelievably generous. Even with their dramas and reconciliations! As strong as they are, remember that they're sensitive and need appreciation. Don't *ever* shame them. *Secret Tip:* Their gifts have to be classy.

☆ But Your Brand-new Friend Is

Your new pal is bossy and exaggerates a lot, but his or her brand of charm is irresistible. You want to be just like this superstar!

☆ But Your Teacher Is

In class, this teacher is like a king holding court. With his or her sense of drama, class is always interesting, if not outright fun. If you have a favorite drama coach, chances are, he or she's a Leo!

☆ But Your Parent Is

Your Leo parent is proud of you and spoils you. The only thing is, your 'rent expects you to behave like him or her, which is hard, 'cos . . . you're different. But Leo parents are also fun and playful, so explain it them, love them, and they'll get it.

☆ But Your Sister or Brother Is

Leo siblings are great because they protect you against anything or anyone that dares threaten you. They're number one with you, even if they *do* grab all the limelight in your family. You know they can't help it. They *are* the limelight.

☆ But Your Pet Is

Your pet is royal, and must be treated as so.
He is affectionate, and only wants three things: your attention, your attention, and your attention! He expects to be boss of your other pets. Let him. (They will. They know who's Lion.)

LEO STAR-JOTTER

LEO STARLETS
Kobe Bryant: August 23, 1978
Erika Christensen: August 19, 1982
Lil' Romeo: August 19, 1989
Anna Paquin: July 24, 1982
Brad Renfro: July 25, 1982

LEO HIGHEST HONORS
Louis Armstrong, inventor of scat, pioneer of swing: August 4, 1901
Amelia Earhart, first woman aviator: July 24, 1898
Alfred Hitchcock, movie director: August 13, 1899

FAVORITE LEO CHARACTERS
Juliet Capulet (*Romeo and Juliet*)
Harry Potter
Lisa Simpson (*The Simpsons*)

VIRGO

VIRGO

YOUR SPECIAL TIME: August 23–September 22

Your birthday is harvesttime! In the days before there were cities, now would be the busiest time, picking all the crops. But even today this is still the busiest time. After a long, lazy summer, you go back to school—to think, learn, and *produce*!

YOUR AWESOME TRAITS

You are real, honest, practical, helpful, and analytical. And you are very, very smart. Your psychic radar picks up every detail! Like the Princess and the Pea, you know when all is not cool—you feel it, even through a ton of feather mattresses. And, like the princess, you won't sleep a wink until you fix it. Speaking of winks, you sleep less than other signs. This is because you're always busy as a bee, thinking, figuring, improving. If only you were president! Instead, you are a teacher and a healer. Virgos give their lives to helping others, like Virgo Mother Teresa, who helped the sick and needy, and Virgo Maria Montessori, a trailblazing children's educator. These kind busy-bee women had to fight to do what they did. The world did not support or approve of them at first. But independent Virgos are known for their sacrifices. For all your strength and integrity, you are modest and humble. You give your all to everything you touch—to your family, your friends, and your schoolwork. Although you have so many gifts, you don't have to save the world, Virgo. But if you want to, you know you can!

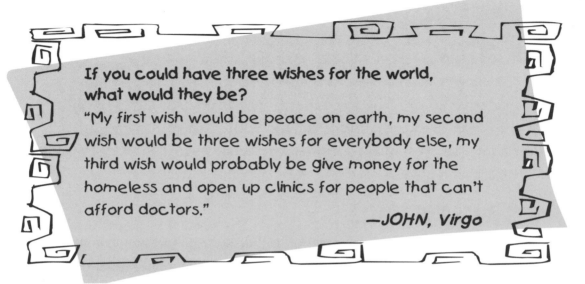

If you could have three wishes for the world, what would they be?

"My first wish would be peace on earth, my second wish would be three wishes for everybody else, my third wish would probably be give money for the homeless and open up clinics for people that can't afford doctors."

—JOHN, Virgo

OF ALL THE ANIMALS, YOU ARE MOST LIKE . . . A Worker Bee

Bees are *very* smart. They know when they land on a flower if it has nectar in it or not, just by sixth-sensing it! And for years, scientists couldn't figure out how bees fly. They said it was a physical impossibility. Virgo accomplishes what the rest of us *think* is impossible. The bee is the busiest, most useful insect of all. It *pollinates*. Without this, many fruits and flowers would not exist. If bees stopped existing, so would animals, crops, and much of our ecosystem.

WHO WAS YOUR VIRGO?

Virgo was the Virgin Astraea. This is where some of your friends say, *virgin*? But *virgin* in the strictest sense means "*purist*." Like puri-fied water, with all chemicals and other impurities removed. Or organic food that is grown naturally, without pesticides or hormones. Astraea preached her pure ideals on Earth during the Golden Age. When she saw we weren't listening, she left Earth and returned to the sky as the constel-lation Virgo. But even from there, she still watches over us.

YOUR RULING PLANET: Brainiac Mercury

Mercury is the star of thought. He is your *brain-sifter, thought-processor* planet. Your busy-bee planet races around the Sun, getting its job done faster than any other planet. A Mercurian year is only 88 days, whereas our Earth year is 365 days. Your Mercury is so busy, too, that we only see him three or four times a year. Earth is about 7,200 miles in diameter, Mercury only 3,000. If Earth were a baseball, Mercury would be a Ping-Pong ball. Just like a Ping-Pong ball, speedy Mercury is busy bouncing brain waves, information, and speech to all Earthlings. But it gives Mercury-ruled Virgo and Gemini the *most*.

WHO WAS YOUR HERMES?

Hermes was a great healer to the ancient Greeks. (Later, the Romans renamed him Mercury, the crazy-fast messenger that's also associated with Gemini. Virgo gets the classic Greek healer version. Gemini gets the newer Roman chatterbox version!) In the ancient pictures, Hermes carries a caduceus. You know that curly symbol you see in doctors' offices and in pharmacies? That's Hermes' caduceus. It is used today by the medical community as the symbol for healing.

THE PART OF YOUR BODY THAT VIRGO RULES:
Your Nervous System and Intestines

Like the bee, who is so sensitive it can taste through its *legs*, you also feel everything. You are a picky eater, feel stress in your stomach, and have more weird diets than any other sign. You also have to watch out for eating disorders more than the other signs.

IN YOUR ELEMENT: Earth

Virgo is an Earth sign. The Earth is our biggest producer—of anything. And of all the signs of the zodiac, so are you! You are earthy, practical, and organized. You toil and turn over the soil for solid, concrete answers until you get the results you want.

YOUR LUCKY . . .

☆ **Colors:** Your lucky colors are navy blue and gray, very cool and classy!

☆ **Metal:** Mercury. From your brainiac star Mercury!

☆ **Precious stone:** Sapphire

☆ **Day of the week:** Wednesday, same as Gemini, because you're both ruled by Mercury! *Mercredi*, in French, is "Wednesday," and is from Mercury. So schedule all the things you want to be lucky on Wednesdays.

IN SCHOOL

Your classmates ask *you* for the right answers. Your brain loves to chew on facts and information. But you can get obsessive and drive yourself too hard. So, whether it's sports or math or writing, take a break sometimes!

WITH YOUR TEACHERS

You're the perfect student and your teachers' fave class monitor. No need to worry about their approval *at all*. (Secretly, though, your teachers wish you would participate in class discussion a *little* bit more.)

ON THE PLAYGROUND

While everyone else is running around letting off steam, you're off quietly doing something interesting with your best friend. And you love to *count* stuff; you get totally absorbed, until it's time to go back to class.

WITH YOUR FRIENDS

You make a passionate friend. You're there for your friends, and they depend on you. You see what's best for them, and you want to help make it happen. But sometimes it's good to chill and see that not everything can be fixed. People make their own choices. That's life!

WITH YOUR FAMILY

Sometimes your family can seem kind of *loud* to you. You like everything just so, and this includes your rituals with your pets. You don't have any? Virgos are the best with pets! If you're allergic, get a turtle, or fish!

TRUE LOVE

You look reserved on the outside, but on the inside you are a deep well of emotion. You take your time choosing who you really like. Only the whole enchilada will do for you.

Best Love Matches: Capricorn, Scorpio, Taurus, Virgo. Sometimes, Aquarius.

WHICH SIGNS YOU GROOVE WITH;
Which Signs You Don't

The easiest signs are the other Earth signs, Capricorn and Taurus, and of course your own, Virgo. You guys all think along the same lines. You and Scorpio both have the same still-waters-run-deep thing going on, so you like one another the first moment you meet. Your next best

friend is Libra, who can criticize everything almost as well as you do! The hardest for you are wacky Sagittarius and bossy Aries. Just let them do their own thing, and you'll laugh together.

HOW TO SPOT A VIRGO

You want someone to help you with something? Find a Virgo. I bet either your doctor, vet, dentist, school nurse, dietician, or janitor is a Virgo: There are more Virgos than any other sign in the health and food professions. They're also the ones edit-

ing the school paper, or making you laugh like Virgo comedian Adam Sandler. They're the athletes, artists, teachers, nurses, vets, doctors, and saints who practice their trade harder than anyone.

Okay, So You're Not a Virgo . . .

☆ But Your Crush Is

Don't be put off if your crush tells you exactly what's wrong with you—that just means they like you! The best thing to do to attract a Virgo love interest is this: Underplay *everything*. Also: Be a good sport. Don't brag. Be smart. Don't push or pry. Be kind to animals. Talk about your pets. And, most important, compliment them! (Leos get all the compliments, Virgos never enough.)

Secret Tip: Virgo boys like to do the chasing. Virgo girls like to be appreciated.

☆ But Your Best Friend Is

Your best friend is your one and only. Virgo best friends make a lot of suggestions, but that's just their way of being *all that*. They know and teach you the best games. At the mall of life, they tell you what works for you and what doesn't, and they find the best bargains. They're always there, whenever you need them.

☆ But Your Brand-new Friend Is

Your new friend seems quiet and intense when the two of you first meet. And don't be surprised if he or she watches shows like *Weakest Link* and *Jeopardy!* Virgos have more info and trivia up their shirtsleeves than anyone!

☆ But Your Teacher Is

Does your teacher say *evidence* a lot? Or *facts* or *real* or *hands on*? Does he or she like to make charts and diagrams to explain everything in total detail? Or go a little crazy if you're late? Must be a Virgo!

☆ But Your Parent Is

Virgos make ultraperfect parents. They're smart and they care. They do the right thing. They want *you* to do the right thing, too (like clean your room one thousand times a week). Their lectures are longer than other parents' lectures, but much *smarter*.

☆ But Your Sister or Brother Is

Virgo siblings seem to do things better than the rest of us, especially Scrabble, Boggle, or puzzles. They love word-plays and figuring stuff out, and can count things for hours. Expect them to nag you, make lists of your chores, and criticize you to your face, but to defend you *fiercely* behind your back.

☆ But Your Pet Is

Your pet is always washing himself. (He also likes to watch you in the shower, too. It's that Virgo cleanliness thing.) He's not a sociable people pet. He's devoted only to you and your family.

VIRGO ASTRO-JOTTER

VIRGO STARLETS
Macaulay Culkin: August 26, 1980
Beyonce Knowles: September 4, 1981
Prince Harry: September 15, 1984
LeAnn Rimes: August 28, 1982
Ben Savage: September 13, 1980

VIRGO HIGHEST HONORS
Mother Teresa, saint: August 27, 1910
Jesse Owens, Olympic athlete: September 12, 1913
Saint Hildegard of Bingen, doctor, composer, writer: August 26, 1098

FAVORITE VIRGO CHARACTERS
Inspector Poirot *(Agatha Christie)*
Tweety Bird
Felix Unger *(The Odd Couple)*

LIBRA

YOUR SPECIAL TIME: September 23–October 22

You are born when day and night hours are perfectly equal. Ah, complete balance! In the old days this was the time of year when scales *ruled*. We weighed crops and grains on scales after harvesting them. In Libra-time, we enjoy the fruits of our labors. Libra *loves* everyone to enjoy.

YOUR AWESOME TRAITS

You are the charmer of the zodiac. You are diplomatic, peace-loving, sensitive, idealistic, appreciative, thoughtful, artistic, sociable, and passionate about justice. You want the world to be beautiful and fair. Like fellow Libras who acted for peace and tolerance—Desmond Tutu, Mahatma Gandhi, John Lennon—you go out of your way to make things better. No one puts others at ease as well as you do. You try for a win-win situation that makes everybody happy. This makes you very popular. In contrast to what most astrologers say, your state of balance and harmony is hard won. It is your greatest *wish*! You must go up and down on the scales a few times to find such a lovely nirvana state. This gives you a fine-tuned analytical mind and a brilliant critical eye. To reach the truth, you take time with your decisions. Your scales must weigh every possibility!

What does astrology mean to you?
"I think it's really neat. You're not just saying it can help you get through life, you can also understand more about it. You understand your personality and other people, and it helps you." —ELIZABETH, Libra

OF ALL THE ANIMALS, YOU ARE MOST LIKE . . . A Cat and a Dog!

As you go from one side of the scale to the other, half the time you are like a dog and half the time you are like a cat. Sociable dogs love to play, and to please their master. They're like an "emotion thermometer." If their human is unhappy, they are unhappy. They need approval more than anything. For Libra humans, it's important to look at this. Sometimes, you must risk peer pressure in order to tell the truth, and do things your own way. Now, as a cat, you are the dog's opposite! You are unto yourself, independent, proud, wise: You let others worship you. Going from one to the other is how you find your balance. Being only one way would dissatisfy you. You need a little of both!

WHO WAS YOUR LIBRA?

Libra was Themis, goddess of Justice. She is the symbol still used in all courts of law today. You have probably seen her—a blindfolded woman holding a pair of scales and a sword. Her purpose is to *feel* justice (that's why she's blindfolded) and to use her sword for sharp reasoning!

YOUR RULING PLANET: Beautiful Venus

Venus is the star of beauty, love, and the sweet life. She is your *love-goddess* planet! The three brightest objects in the solar system are the Sun, the Moon, and Venus, and at night you can see Venus shining right next to the Moon. Hottie Venus has the highest temperatures next to the Sun: 900 degrees Fahrenheit. She is the *only* planet that is a complete and perfect sphere. Wonderfully balanced, just like perfect, beautiful Libra! The light of the Sun reflects beautifully on her clouds. Venus's energy gives Earthlings the desire for beauty, love, and pleasure. She gives Libra the most.

WHO WAS YOUR VENUS?

The ancient Greeks wrote that Venus was so beautiful, flowers grew wherever she walked. She was so enchanting that she "stole the wits even of the wise." This goddess of love and beauty was worshiped in many societies. (The Greeks called her Aphrodite.) Venus is a *muse*, and through the ages she has been an inspiration to many artists. The oldest image of Venus ever discovered, the famous figurine called the *Venus of Willendorf*, is 27,000 to 32,000 years old. And one of the most famous representations of Venus is Botticelli's painting *The Birth of Venus*.

THE PART OF YOUR BODY THAT LIBRA RULES:
Your Skin, Veins, Kidneys, and Lower Back

All that Libra rules is about balance and harmony.

The skin: It is like a Libra thermometer. Disturbances in your body show up on the skin.

The veins: You rule them because they are the vessels that lead to the *heart*.

The kidneys: They are the filter or go-between. As in life, you act as filters or go-betweens. You need to drink lots of water to prevent kidney stones.

The lower back: It hurts from pressure. This means emotional pressure, too.

IN YOUR ELEMENT: Air

You are an air sign. Air rules thought. Air signs are smart and fantastic with words and ideas. But just because you're an attractive Venusian, don't let anyone call you an *airhead*—you're too smart for that!

YOUR LUCKY . . .

☆ **Colors:** Your lucky colors are sky blue, magenta, and lavender.
☆ **Metal:** Copper.
☆ **Precious stone:** Opal. This stone is lucky only for Libras.
☆ **Day of the week:** Friday. *Vendredi* is French for "Friday" and comes from Venus. So schedule everything you want to be lucky on Fridays.

IN SCHOOL

As long as your classes and teachers are interesting, you're in heaven. You love rules and structure, but you're quick to question something if it doesn't seem right to you. Be careful of your tendency to procrastinate and leave things to the last minute.

WITH YOUR TEACHERS

You want your teacher to be right and fair, and you're supersensitive to their approval. Sometimes you need them to push you to work harder. You're a natural debater, and like to interact.

ON THE PLAYGROUND

You care about being popular, so you're usually part of the "in" crowd. You can get into trends, and can be a slave to fashion. You don't like gossip, and your sense of justice makes you defend the underdog.

WITH YOUR FRIENDS

You have a lot of friends from different groups. You get along with just about everybody! You like it when everyone's happy together. Friends come to you with love problems *all* the time.

WITH YOUR FAMILY

The most important thing to you is that no one's yelling. That disturbs you and makes you shut down and not want to talk. You love to talk with your family and you love their stories. You're the only sign who's *really* into how your house is put together. Colors, music, and peace are key.

TRUE LOVE

You idealize and dream about love nonstop. You have a million crushes, and they change pretty fast, but each one feels like it. You have a ton of admirers, but some might be too shy to talk to you. **Best Love Matches:** Gemini, Aquarius, Libra, and Leo. Sometimes Aries.

WHICH SIGNS YOU GROOVE WITH; Which Signs You Don't

The easiest signs are the other air signs: Aquarius, Gemini, and of course your own, Libra. You all think alike, and you all think a *lot*. Virgo and Taurus can be too direct, sometimes. The hardest for you are wet-blanket Cancer and bossy Aries—though you can have fun with Aries. You'll be so much happier with your Cancer friends if you remember that it's in the crab's nature to go up and down, just like the tides. Learn to leave them alone a little more, relax, and make them laugh—they love jokes. You're more than up to the task, Libra: Because you're good at seeing different sides of people, you get along with more signs than anyone.

HOW TO SPOT A LIBRA

If it's a trillion sweaty degrees outside, look for those aliens who look clean and cool! The Libra face and expression is always nice and calm, even if they're acting out a tragedy. Libra Gwyneth Paltrow is a perfect example of this. If you do your sleuth-looking right, you'll even see nice Libra Marshall Mathers under bad-boy Eminem. Typical Libra faces are perfectly oval or round. Libras Kate Winslet, Alicia Silverstone, Matt Damon, Janeane Garofalo, Gwen Stefani, and Ziggy Marley all have *curvy*

faces. Due to Venus's beauty spell, extra weight looks good on them! They have good skin, too, as Libra rules the skin. Now, not to judge a book by its cover, you can also spot a Libra in a crowd by checking out who's debating, who's listening the most to others, who's arguing for justice, and who's smiling the most—all at once!

Okay, So You're Not a Libra . . .

☆ But Your Crush Is

He or she is probably *really* good-looking, but have you ever actually *sat down* with your Libra crush? Libras change seats a million times. It has to feel right and be the right atmosphere, or they're miserable. They're very sensitive and like to flirt. **Secret Tips:** Look your best. Don't be rude. Don't look around when you're talking to them. They'll say, "You're not listening!" Brush up on your compliments and little gestures. They're important!

☆ But Your Best Friend Is

Libra best friends are either talking you into something or calming you down. They compare everyone. It's not personal; it's just their scales weighing all the differences they find. They're generous and will go out of their way to help you. They're thinking about their crush nonstop.

☆ But Your Brand-new Friend Is

Your new friend makes you feel great. When you talk, he or she listens to you like you're the last person on Earth. But by the end of any given day at school he or she has made a dozen new friends, so your plans together often have to change at the last-minute.

☆ But Your Teacher Is

Teachers who are Libras try to treat everyone fairly and to entertain the class. They laugh a lot, and give opinions, facts, and stories all in one class. They're also a lot better dressed than all the other teachers!

☆ But Your Parent Is

Libra parents want you to look nice and have responsible friends and good grades. They insist on manners and a neat, beautiful home. They *love* discussions at the dinner table. If you want to change the subject, say the magic word *fair*. It works a spell on them! They also like fun and parties.

☆ But Your Sister or Brother Is

Libra siblings want to hang out with you, have fun, and for you to help them. When they argue, they say, "That's not fair!" a lot. They hog the bathroom *and* your music.

☆ But Your Pet Is

Libra pets are really into grooming themselves, even the dogs. They're also very affectionate; even the cats like other cats. You must entertain and pet them constantly.

LIBRA ASTRO-JOTTER

LIBRA STARLETS
Kieran Culkin: September 30, 1982
Zachery Hanson: October 22, 1985
Martina Hingis: September 30, 1980
Jonathan Lipnicki: October 22, 1991
Serena Williams: September 26, 1981

LIBRA HIGHEST HONORS
Mahatma Gandhi, peace leader: October 2, 1869
Mickey Mantle, baseball player: October 20, 1931
Eleanor Roosevelt, first lady and activist: October 11, 1884

FAVORITE LIBRA CHARACTERS
Marcia Brady (*The Brady Bunch*)
Charlie Brown (*Peanuts*)
Dr. Beverly Crusher (*Star Trek: Starship Enterprise*)

SCORPIO

SCORPIO

YOUR SPECIAL TIME: October 23–November 21

Your sign is the sign of *transformation*. You are born with the falling of the leaves; like a snake shedding its skin, nature is already moving on to the next chapter.

YOUR AWESOME TRAITS

Your power, like the unconscious, which is 90 percent of our brain activity, is very deep. What others see of you is only the tip of the iceberg. You are

determined, protective, empathic, brilliant, magnetic, athletic, focused, self-sufficient, and strong *and* sensitive. You're also brave, unbreakable, loyal, and open-minded. You have many choices in life because your sign has not just one but *three* symbols! You are a true wizard—if you want to be. You can accomplish almost anything you set out to do. You are called the Zodiac Detective, because you can figure out stuff the rest of us find mysterious. Many brilliant scientists, especially those exploring space, have been Scorpios: Carl Sagan, Edwin Hubble, and Edmund Halley, just to name a few. You have hidden psychic gifts and will leave a great mark on the world.

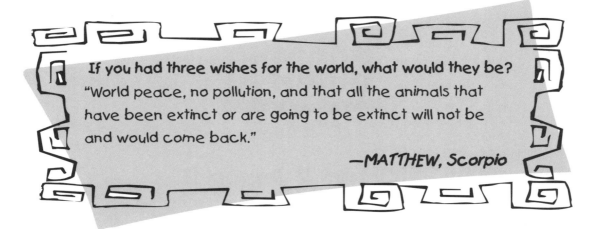

If you had three wishes for the world, what would they be?
"World peace, no pollution, and that all the animals that have been extinct or are going to be extinct will not be and would come back."

—MATTHEW, Scorpio

OF ALL THE ANIMALS, YOU ARE MOST LIKE
. . . An Eagle and a Phoenix and a Scorpion!

Scorpio is so powerful, it has three very different choices. *You* choose the one you want to be in your life: the protective eagle, the magical phoenix, or the vengeful scorpion. The eagle soars high and proud, protecting its loved ones. America uses the eagle as its symbol, and Native Americans—the original Americans—also considered the eagle to be *their* strongest symbol: of healing. The phoenix is a bird that has incredible magical powers and the ability to rebirth itself through great challenge. And finally, the scorpion expects fierce loyalty—and seeks revenge when betrayed!

WHO WAS YOUR SCORPIO?

Because you have three symbols, you get to have three myths! One is the myth of the phoenix. A legendary bird that burned itself to ashes, then rose alive from the ashes to live again, its story is all about unvanquished strength and magical power. The second myth is that of the scorpion. Legend has it that

Diana, the Moon-goddess, brought a giant scorpion out of the Earth to sting the giant Orion, who had attacked her. Thus the scorpion symbolizes self-defense and self- protection. Finally, the third myth uses the serpent to represent ancient wisdom and strength. The modern version of all these symbols is the eagle.

YOUR RULING PLANET: Proud Pluto

Pluto is the star of transformation. It is the only planet that spacecraft haven't explored yet. Pluto is cold and dark, so distant it takes 248 years to orbit the Sun. Despite being so far away, Pluto's power on us is awesome. It affects earthquakes and volcanoes, endings and beginnings, and our unconscious. It was given its name by a young British girl. Her letter was the first to arrive at the Lowell Observatory, where Pluto was discovered in 1930. Before this, it was nameless and mysterious. It was called Planet X. . . .

WHO WAS YOUR PLUTO?

Pluto, aka Hades, was King of the Underworld. He lived there alone for years until he fell in love with Persephone, stole her, and took her down below. Her mother, Demeter, goddess of fertility, was so sad at losing her daughter that the whole Earth went into mourning. Nothing grew, and everyone started to die! Finally, they made a deal. Persephone could live above ground for half the year with her parents, and the other half with her husband, Pluto. This is why half the year the Earth is barren (winter and fall), and half the year it is fertile (spring and summer). And why Pluto is only happy *half* the time.

THE PART OF YOUR BODY THAT SCORPIO RULES:
Your Reproductive Organs

Scorpio is all about birth and rebirth, so it makes sense that Scorpio rules our reproductive organs. Without these, we couldn't be born. And Scorpios need to take extra care with their reproductive organs.

IN YOUR ELEMENT: Water

Scorpio is a water sign, like Cancer and Pisces. Water rules the unconscious. Still waters run deep in you. This is where you get your reputation for brilliance. You explore the deep end!

YOUR LUCKY . . .

☆ **Colors:** Your lucky colors are crimson and black, the colors of passion and power.

☆ **Metal:** Plutonium. Plutonium is from Pluto and can never be destroyed.

☆ **Precious stone:** Topaz

☆ **Day of the week:** Tuesday, which you share with Aries. Scorpio and Aries are the only signs who never quit (even when it might make more sense to do so!). Schedule all things you want to be lucky on Tuesdays.

IN SCHOOL

Here is where you have total choice. You can either be top honor student, head of your class, or waste your time goofing off. However, when you find a subject that fascinates you, you always go all the way. Science, sports, literature, and music are particular faves.

WITH YOUR TEACHERS

You love to find out stuff, so your teachers had better be ready for your questions! As long as they don't force you down any particular path, you love them, and they love *you*.

ON THE PLAYGROUND

Though you look so calm on the outside, you have a lot of pent-up energy to get out. You're ultra-active, running around with other kids, or off investigating and exploring a secret mystery. You like to do this on your own, or maybe with one person you can trust not to tell!

WITH YOUR FRIENDS

You're wise for your years, so you seem older than most of your peers. There are only one or two friends you *really* let in. These are special, and you'll stay friends with them forever. The rest are good for fun and laughs.

WITH YOUR FAMILY

You respect your family. You pick up what they're feeling without them having to say a word. You love them fiercely, but you won't always know it. You need a lot of privacy for yourself.

TRUE LOVE

Whew! It's all or nothing with you. You have secret crushes that you can think about for years. And they don't even know about it! Try to tell them that, okay? **Best Love Matches:** Virgo, Cancer, Pisces, and Taurus

WHICH SIGNS YOU GROOVE WITH; Which Signs You Don't

The easiest signs for you are Capricorn, Scorpio, Aries, and Pisces. You guys think a lot alike, and have fun going on adventures together. You're drawn to Leo and Libra, even though they can make you impatient with all their talk about me, me, me. Gemini and Aquarius get you down, though. They're so all over the place, you spend a lot of your time with them doing damage-control!

HOW TO SPOT A SCORPIO

If you put out your psychic antennae, you can spot a Scorpio instantly. It's their aura. They're alone, always alone, even when they're with a group of friends. They're thinking about something, but you can't tell what. And they won't give you a clue. They'll just keep thinking. (Their deep thoughtfulness is intriguing and mysterious, and you can bet you'll want to find out what it's all about. But it's *never* what you think it is!) Their faces look like beautiful masks, giving nothing away. They also have big liquid eyes, like Scorpios Julia Roberts and Meg Ryan.

Okay, So You're Not a Scorpio . . .

☆ **But Your Crush Is**

Run for your life, babeee! Unless you want to lie awake at nights obsessing. It would be better do your homework and forget this crush. But you can't. Arm yourself if you decide to proceed. Scorpios can say some harsh things and don't mean a thing. You recover when they make you laugh. ***Secret Tip:*** Hold their hand. It calms them.

☆ **But Your Best Friend Is**

Your best friend is kind of groovy! Your number-one pal teaches you about how to boost your self-worth, and you can tell him or her anything. You're always blown away to see that nothing shocks them; it opens new worlds to you. Your best friend is compassionate, too.

☆ **But Your Brand-new Friend Is**

Scorpios don't make new friends easily. They keep you at arm's length for a while, so they can check you out. So you'll only see them once in a while during your "probationary" period. But once you're in, you're in for good.

☆ **But Your Teacher Is**

Scorpio teacher's have genius tendencies, but they also have a unique way of teaching that doesn't always work for you. But if you observe them carefully, you will learn more than you would in a regular class. They say brilliant and truthful things. You just have to be open and receptive!

☆ But Your Parent Is

Scorpios are known for holding a grudge *forever*. But this only applies to strangers and people who *aren't* their family, friends, and pets, so you don't have to worry about seeing this nasty streak in your parents. Sure, they're angry for a little while, but

they get over it. And they won't hold it against you! They're strong, authoritative figures, but they're very loving, too. Nobody takes care of you better!

☆ But Your Sister or Brother Is

Your sibling's second name is really "Don'tcomeintomyroom." If you ever do come in, the room is like a monk's room: It's so bare, you never see anything anyway! Your Scorpio sib never betrays a secret. He or she is also good for listening to music with, and taking you to new places.

☆ But Your Pet Is

Your pet is only pretending to be a pet. That sweet kitty is really a panther in the raw. Walking across your living room like he or she is stalking prey in the Brazilian jungle. Watching you like you could be their next antelope. If you have a dog, expect howling at the full moon. Your very own wolf!

SCORPIO ASTRO-JOTTER

SCORPIO STARLETS
Lauren Ambrose: November 16, 1978
Lucas Black: November 21, 1982
Rory Culkin: November 8, 1989
Isaac Hanson: November 17, 1980
Sisqo: November 9, 1978

SCORPIO HIGHEST HONORS
Marie Curie, scientist: November 7, 1867
Pablo Picasso, artist: October 25, 1881
Saint Augustine, philosopher, writer: November 13, 354

FAVORITE SCORPIO CHARACTERS
Jan Brady (*The Brady Bunch*)
James Bond
Darth Vader (*Star Wars*)

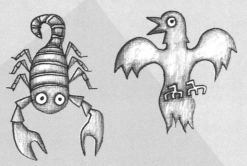

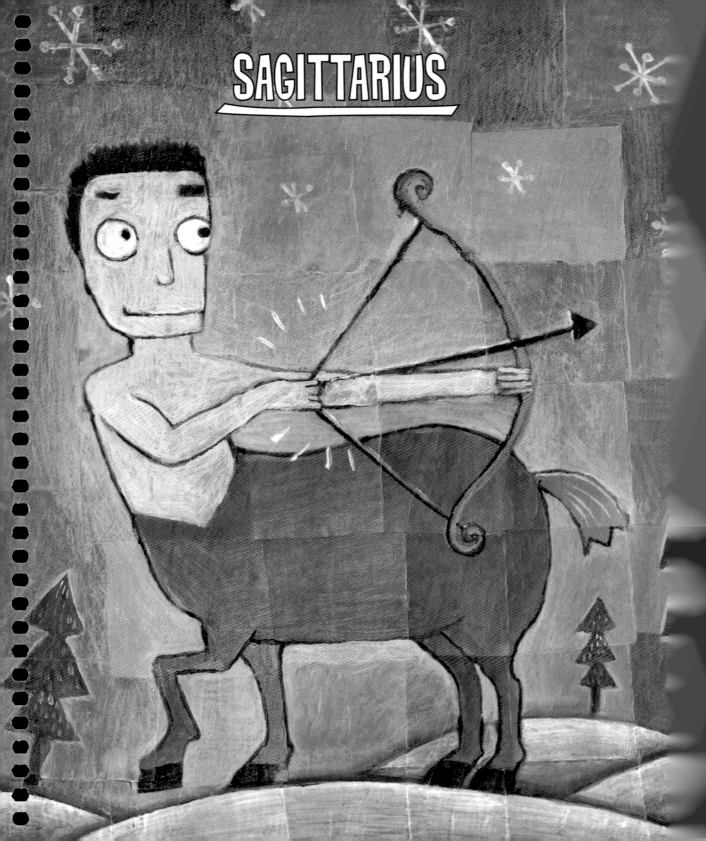

SAGITTARIUS

YOUR SPECIAL TIME: November 22–December 21

It's holiday time! Sagittarius is coming to town, bearing excitement and gifts, and getting us psyched for Thanksgiving, Hanukkah, Christmas, and Kwanzaa— all the major gift-giving days. This is such a great time of year, so much fun and so exciting—just like you, Sagittarius!

YOUR AWESOME TRAITS

You are wow-enthusiastic and love to take risks. You are open, adventurous, creative, fun, funny, impulsive, kind, idealistic, and independent. *Doing it my way* is your own personal slogan, just like fellow Sagittarius Frank Sinatra sang. You aim high with your goals and ambitions. You shoot your arrows into the air and follow them wherever and as far as they go. You are on a constant quest for the truth. You tell it how you see it. Like the child in *The Emperor's New Clothes*, you're the one to blurt out, "But he's not *wearing* any clothes!" You see the big picture and you want to plunge into it.

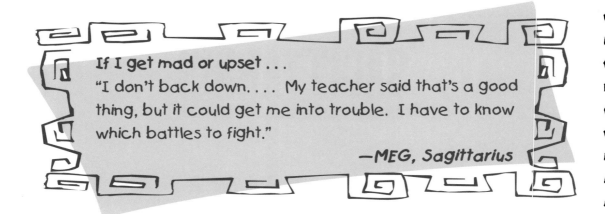

If I get mad or upset . . .
"I don't back down. . . . My teacher said that's a good thing, but it could get me into trouble. I have to know which battles to fight."

—MEG, Sagittarius

OF ALL THE ANIMALS, YOU'RE MOST LIKE . . . A Horse

Sagittarius is the centaur, a magical beast who is half-human and half-horse. Imagine a horse galloping through an open pasture. This beautiful and spirited creature is all strength, speed, and power. Horses want to run wild and free, like you, Sagittarius!

WHO WAS YOUR SAGITTARIUS CENTAUR?

You weren't just any centaur! You were Chiron, the kindest centaur. Chiron was a great healer and teacher, and Hercules was one of his students. One day Hercules accidentally shot Chiron in the thigh during a hunting lesson. Chiron was immortal, so he could not die. But he chose give up his immortality to Jupiter in order to free Prometheus, the giver of fire. In return for giving fire back to the world, Jupiter rewarded the centaur by placing him among the stars, and he became the constellation Sagittarius.

YOUR RULING PLANET: Generous Giant Jupiter

Jupiter is your *lotto winner* planet. Unlike the other planets, which take energy from the Sun, Jupiter *gives*. It emits its own energy, so it is its own miniature sun, with its own solar system, and a family of sixteen moons. And it protects. Scientists say that Jupiter has been keeping destroyer asteroids off Earth for millenniums. Its gravitational field just pulls them off course, and deflects them back into space! Jupiter is bigger than, and weighs twice as much as, all the other planets *combined*. It has a hurricane called the Great Red Spot that is always going and is big enough to hold two Earths. Jupiter's energy is always going, too, offering us the chance to be lucky, good, and happy. But that's no surprise—its atmosphere is made mostly of laughing gas (helium).

WHO WAS YOUR JUPITER?

He was first called Zeus by the Greeks and then Jupiter, or Jove, by the Romans. Jove is where we get the word "jovial" from. Jovial means joyful, playful, and full humor. Jupiter was ruler of *all* the gods. And both Greeks and Romans believed Jupiter to be just and merciful. He was the supreme lawgiver and spiritual chief of Rome.

THE PART OF YOUR BODY THAT SAGITTARIUS RULES:
Your Liver, Hips, and Thighs

You need to watch rich food and drink intake because you get hepatitis (of the liver) more than other signs. You are always on the go, too—and aren't your *hips* and *thighs* necessary to run? So watch out for accidents.

IN YOUR ELEMENT: Fire

A fire sign needs its freedom. Fire cannot be contained (and in you, least of all!). Fire spreads feelings, ideas, excitement, and the rush of pure joy!

YOUR LUCKY . . .

☆ **Colors:** Your lucky colors are purple and silver, the colors of royalty and magic.

☆ **Metal:** Tin (Like the Tin Man who wanted a heart only to discover he had the most heart of all!)

☆ **Precious stone:** Turquoise, which protects and gives the ability to see into the future

☆ **Day of the week:** Thursday. "Thursday" in French is *jeudi*, which comes from Jove and Jupiter. So schedule all things you want to be lucky on Thursdays.

IN SCHOOL

You're quick and full of ideas. You take great leaps in class discussions. And you're *lucky* (thank Jupiter for that!), so you can study at the last minute and still ace your tests. To be a star, all you need is staying power to finish a project before you gallop off to meet the next challenge.

WITH YOUR TEACHERS

If your teachers believe in freedom of speech like you do, you get on great with them. But you have a tough time with those rule-loving taskmasters. You love to ask why. Your teachers have to realize that you follow ideas, like your arrows, as far as they will take you. And then you go even further!

ON THE PLAYGROUND

You're restless, fearless, and curious. You're either talking to a million different people, or leading your gang off into an adventure. Be careful of accidents, though. You bump, fall, and bruise more than anyone except an Aries ram!

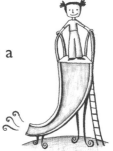

WITH YOUR FRIENDS

You're a great friend to have because you don't make friendship an *obligation* thing. You have all sorts of different friends whom you think are equally great. You're also trusting. Because of this, sometimes you get teased.

WITH YOUR FAMILY

You like lots of affection in your family. As you get older, you may wander off and travel a lot, but while you're at home, this is the way you like it.

TRUE LOVE

When you fall in love, it's head over heels. But sooner or later, it's time for your adventurous spirit to move on. Only somebody who keeps you laughing, or always on your toes, will bring out your staying power.

Best Love Matches: Aquarius, Aries, Leo, Gemini, and sometimes your own, Sagittarius.

WHICH SIGNS YOU GROOVE WITH; Which Signs You Don't

The easiest signs for you are your fellow fire signs, Aries, Leo, and Sagittarius, because you guys all love to have fun and go on adventures. Your next best friends are air signs, Aquarius, Gemini, and Libra. Scorpio's

interesting, but for you, Capricorn and Taurus can be downright boring. Capricorn can make you laugh hysterically, but they're a little too concerned with peer approval and you want them to lighten up about that. And Taurus wants to stay still—a problem since you always want to be on the move. The worst for you are Virgo and Pisces; they can be way too critical and clingy! But they're great for getting you in order, though—like making sure you finish your homework!

HOW TO SPOT A SAGITTARIUS

Sagittarians always stand out: They're the ones arguing a cause, telling some truth about society, or losing their head over somebody. You'll definitely notice them! The ones who tell the truth  about society do it dramatically, like Steven Spielberg or Jimi Hendrix; humorously, like Woody Allen; or way over the top, like Sinéad O'Connor. They like to own dogs, so you find them in parks. In fact, they're big animal-lovers all around, so look in animal shelters and zoos, too. Interestingly enough, many Sagittarians are tennis players. (It might be that bow-and-arrow thing transformed into a modern-day tennis racket!) Some famous Sagittarius tennis pros are Monica Seles, Billie Jean King, Boris Becker, and Chris Evert. Sagittarians have short attention spans (perfect for following a tennis ball!), so they'll never be where you found them a second ago. Wherever they are and whatever they are doing, they are *not* sitting still.

☆ But Your Crush Is

It's so easy to start a conversation with Sagittarians! They love to talk. Mention animals, or a new way-out idea, and you can't go wrong. Keep it casual. (Remember, they're the only sign who calls themselves by a zodiac nickname— "Sadge." Never Sagittarius! That's too preten-tious-sounding for them.) If you make a date, count on them to break it at least once. **Secret Tip:** They forget all the time. Their personal song should be "Oops! I Did It Again" sung by fellow Sagittarius Britney Spears.

☆ But Your Best Friend Is

Sagittarian best friends are true originals! When you go the mall, they treat you, spend all their money in the first hour, then ask to borrow. Just remember how generous they are when you run out. **Secret tip:** Whatever you do, *don't* judge their other friends.

☆ But Your Brand-new Friend Is

You find your new pal exciting, if not a little strange. He or she wants to be your friend, but doesn't want to be in touch all the time. This might seem arrogant, but don't take it personally. Your new friend is very enthusiastic about you and even gives you surprise gifts!

☆ But Your Teacher Is

Your Sagittarius teacher is passionate about teaching, the world, and *you*. He or she believes in causes; they might be your best teacher ever.

☆ But Your Parent Is

Your parent is more fun than most parents, and encourages you to be independent and to go after your goals. He or she lets you do your own thing, even argue with your sibling, as long as you "take it outside." Sadge parents also love parties and going on travel vacations.

☆ But Your Sister or Brother Is

Your sibling out-runs and out-jokes everyone. He or she is always bouncing around and knocking things off tables. (No, this is not the pet section. Your sib is just active—and a little clumsy!)

☆ But Your Pet Is

Even the cats are clumsy! The dogs are super-affectionate and give you huge sloppy kisses. Both love to run free, even when they're old.

SAGITTARIUS ASTRO-JOTTER

SAGITTARIUS STARLETS
Christina Aguilera: December 18, 1980
Aaron Carter: December 7, 1987
Anna Chlumsky: December 3, 1980
Katie Holmes: December 18, 1978
Britney Spears: December 2, 1981

SAGITTARIUS HIGHEST HONORS
Joe Di Maggio, baseball player: November 25, 1914
Charles Schulz, *Peanuts* creator: November 26, 1922
Mark Twain, writer and humorist: November 30, 1832

FAVORITE SAGITTARIUS CHARACTERS
Barney
Huckleberry Finn (*Tom Sawyer*)
Bart Simpson (*The Simpsons*)

CAPRICORN

YOUR SPECIAL TIME: December 22–January 19

You are born during the most challenging time of the year. The trees and ground are bare, and it is time to squirrel away and save for the future. Despite ancient fears about survival, there is faith and hope. *You* are being born! There is birth and life even in the dead of winter. You are practical. You go forward, and up. You come out on top. You are the Winter Winner.

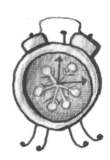

YOUR AWESOME TRAITS

Your secret power, Capricorn sea-goat, is that you can adapt to anything, even water. That's because the sea-goat originally came from water! But you are 75 percent goat and only 25 percent fish, so your true purpose is to triumph on *land*, to reach the mountaintop with all your goals accomplished. You are wise, rational, determined, driven, modest, intensely loyal to your family and friends, and have a hysterical sense of humor. You are like Capricorn Tiger Woods who endured racial barriers to become a golf legend—before the age of twenty-five! Or like Capricorn Joan of Arc, who, when she was seventeen years old, led the French army against the British and won! Capricorns also are the best planners. Remember it was Capricorn Paul Revere who warned American colonists, "The British are coming, the British are coming!" And it was Capricorn Betsy Ross who sewed the American flag, which has served as our symbol now for over two hundred years. Finally, Goat Jim Carrey wrote a check to himself for *ten million dollars* when he was poor and working with his parents in a factory. He was able to cash it a few years ago. He knew he would (talk about being driven!).

OF ALL THE ANIMALS, YOU ARE MOST LIKE . . . A Mountain Goat

The goat was created to survive. Its thick wool protects it from the mountain's low temperatures at high altitudes. The soft pads on the bottom of its feet act as suction cups, and its toes act like pliers as it moves up steep ledges. It maneuvers precarious paths and ledges that would kill other animals. It makes leaps of thirty feet to small ledges that are barely wide enough to stand on! The goat is born knowing how to stretch and reach for new heights and goals. It always lands on its feet.

WHO WAS YOUR SEA-GOAT?

Over six thousand years ago there was a magnificent sea-goat named Ea. He was a famous teacher and brought civilization to the people of Mesopotamia. He lived in the ocean under the Earth. Every day he came out to give his wisdom to the people, and every night he returned to his underground sea.

Thousands of years passed, and the Romans and Greeks brought the sea-goat onto land for good. He became Pan, the god of nature, who played the most beautiful music in the world on his reed pipes. Thus, Capricorn, you have two brilliant sides of you: teacher and creator.

YOUR RULING PLANET: Wise Savior Saturn

Saturn is the star of wisdom and lessons. She is your *do-it-right-or-else* planet. Saturn is so light that if you dropped it in water, it would float. It certainly keeps *you* afloat! It has seven rings that stretch out 170,000 miles. Far-reaching, like the rippling effect of *your* actions. Eighteen moons also circle Saturn, moving through the rings. The Greeks called Saturn the Sun of the Night. This may be why you are nocturnal; you're at your best late at night, while the rest of the world is sleeping.

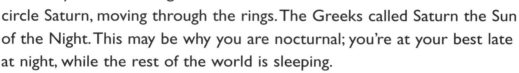

WHO WAS YOUR SATURN?

Saturn was the god of agriculture in Roman times. They celebrated him by partying for eight days straight during the festival of Saturnalia! Saturn was so revered because he brought in the harvest—literally and figuratively. (As in what you put in something is what you'll get out of it. Karma-time!) The earlier Greeks called him Cronus, which means "time." But for the Greeks, Cronus was a more serious god, and it is his influence that causes many Capricorns to fear the loss of time. The good news is that Capricorns get younger the older they get! It's the only sign to do this. You're like old wise men when you're born, but as you age you become irresistibly kid-like.

THE PART OF YOUR BODY THAT CAPRICORN RULES:
Your Teeth, Bones, Knees, and Joints

Capricorn rules our foundation; that is, the very bare
bones of us! Capricorns themselves have beautiful bone
structure, but they always seem to have a blow-out with
their teeth! So they need lots of calcium in order to keep
their bones and teeth strong. They also need plenty of
exercise. But be careful running because of pressure on
the knees. Try yoga instead!

IN YOUR ELEMENT: Earth

You are an Earth sign. Because you are a goat, having
your feet on the ground is your survival. But water
equals dreaming, feeling, and intuition—and you have a
lot of all three! That's where the fish part of you kicks in.
So don't be fooled: Capricorn has two elements, not
just one. It's the only sign of the zodiac that does.

"I relate to being a mystical sea-goat because I like
dolphins. But I also like the mountains and I like to go
on hikes and I love to swim!"

—SCOTT, Capricorn

YOUR LUCKY . . .

☆ **Colors:** Your lucky colors are granite gray, brown,
and dark green. The natural colors of the earth.

☆ **Metal:** Lead

☆ **Precious stone:** Garnet

☆ **Day of the week:** Saturday. This one's easy: Satur-day from Saturn. So, schedule the things you want to be lucky on Saturdays.

IN SCHOOL

You are concerned about grades and about what your teachers think of you. But you do so well! You're painstaking about homework, and you have an incredible eye for detail. When you gather all the facts, the results spell S-U-C-C-E-S-S!

WITH YOUR TEACHERS

Your grades are excellent, but your teachers want you to *share* more in class! You're a quiet, serious thinker and you study hard. You love numbers and philosophy and science. So let's hear about it!

ON THE PLAYGROUND

You don't always remember to *play*: you're always thinking of wonderful things to do or how people are reacting to you. Relax more!

WITH YOUR FRIENDS

You have pretty high standards: You're a good friend and you expect the same from others. You tell some mighty funny jokes, and your friends love you for it.

WITH YOUR FAMILY

Your room has to be perfect. You try to please your parents, but at the same time you need your independence and your space, too. Plus, you can't stand parents who *snoop*! You stay close to your family all of your life, even if you move far away.

TRUE LOVE

You're looking for a go-getter who will be your true soul mate and companion. You want them to be even more powerful than you are, if that's possible. At the very least, they have to be an *equal* leader. Not to mention outright gorgeous!

Best Love Matches: Virgo, Scorpio, Taurus, and Cancer

WHICH SIGNS YOU GROOVE WITH;
Which Signs You Don't

You work best with Scorpio. You *play* best with Leo or Aquarius. But the one that really, *really* rings your bell is Cancer. It's hard with Cancer, but worth it. You can finally relax. Except for Virgo and Taurus, everyone else is so stressed all the time, it's hard.

HOW TO SPOT A CAPRICORN

Look for the person most in control of the room. Capricorns are relaxed and comfortable. They're either making everyone laugh with their jokes,  or holding an audience in *some* way. They usually have pointed features and will look and act a little older than most of their peers. (Unless, of course, they're *really* old—and then they act like kids!) They don't have to prove anything, although they do tend to criticize those around them if they're at a large gathering. Capricorns are all stars-in-the-making.

OKAY, SO YOU'RE NOT A CAPRICORN . . .

☆ **But Your Crush Is**

You can't tell what your crush is thinking. He or she has a natural reserve and is also very choosy. Capricorns can wait forever to find the right mate if they have to, so be patient! They might not act like they need love, but they do! *Secret Tip:* You have to like their family. And never, ever be late for a date.

☆ **But Your Best Friend Is**

Capricorn best friends stick around when the going is toughest. These are seriously great friends. But it might take you a year or two to figure it out.

☆ **But Your Brand-new Friend Is**

You think there's wonderful stuff to be discovered under that cool and trendy surface. And you're right: Underneath, your new pal is genuine, and the realest friend you could ever hope for.

☆ **But Your Teacher Is**

Oh, this teacher makes you work so hard! And his or her comments and grades can come across a little harsh. (It's for your own good, your teacher says!) But Capricorn teachers are patient with you and just want to make sure you learn what you need to.

☆ But Your Parent Is

This parent has great ambitions for you. Capricorn moms and dads plan out your life and express their love through worrying. It's so comforting to them! But remind them to run around and have fun with you, too. You can look forward to growing up with them, though; they loosen up a lot as they get older.

☆ But Your Sister or Brother Is

Your brother or sister has laser-beam focus and can work through anything: music, fights, *anything*! He or she is competitive, but cares deeply about you. (Though your sib will never say exactly how much!)

☆ But Your Pet Is

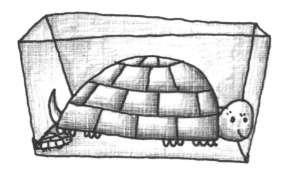

Your pet is boss. Cat, dog, turtle, iguana even. I know a turtle who's a Capricorn. She's grown so large, she's forced her little husband against the sides of their turtle glass home. There's not enough room for him. Like this Capricorn terror, your pet probably likes to throw his or her weight around, too.

CAPRICORN ASTRO-JOTTER

CAPRICORN STARLETS
Jessica Andrews: December 29, 1983
Brynn Elms: January 6, 1987
A. J. McLean: January 9, 1978
Tiger Woods: December 30, 1975
Matthew Yeo: December 30, 1980

CAPRICORN HIGHEST HONORS
Martin Luther King, Jr., civil rights activist: January 15, 1929
Sir Isaac Newton, astronomer: December 25, 1642
Saint Joan of Arc, teenage visionary: January 6, 1412

FAVORITE CAPRICORN CHARACTERS
Thelma (*Scooby Doo*)
The Little Engine That Could
Ebeneezer Scrooge *and* Tiny Tim (*A Christmas Carol*)

AQUARIUS

AQUARIUS

YOUR SPECIAL TIME: January 20–February 19

You are born during the most extreme part of winter—the real thing, before it gets straggly and tired. Before we're *only* waiting for spring. The very heart of winter: This is your time.

YOUR AWESOME TRAITS

You are rebellious, intuitive, truth-telling, brilliant, analytical, determined, idealistic, fun, original, creative, independent, curious, friendly, and unprejudiced. Aquarians see life very simply, with very brilliant minds. It gives you X-ray vision, and also makes you a powerful leader. You're the one to lead animal rights (more vegetarians are Aquarians than any other sign), people rights (Rosa Parks and Abraham Lincoln were both Aquarians!), and environmental rights. Aquarian Julia Butterfly Hill, when she was only twenty-two, gave three years of her life to saving California wildlife from Pacific Lumber. How did she do this? In a typically shocking Aquarius way: She climbed to the top of a redwood tree and didn't come down for three years! You do things in an individualist way. You don't care what other people think, or what the trend is.

OF ALL THE ANIMALS, YOU ARE MOST LIKE . . . A Crane

Cranes are the most beautiful prehistoric waterbirds. They have an ancient history, with great knowledge from the past. They soar independent and serene, then swoop down like a bullet to the water. Their wingspan is ten feet long. Their legs are like those of grasshoppers. They have long, long beaks and inquisitive eyes. Just like Aquarian human eyes, they twinkle. Because they almost became extinct a few years ago, they are secretive about where they rear their babies.

WHO WAS YOUR AQUARIUS?

One day, Jupiter, king of the world, aka Aquarius, looked at the world and decided to create a new race. He and Neptune created the Great Flood. Only two people survived: Deucalion and Pyrrha. They walked, casting stones behind them. Each stone turned into a person. They became the new race of Aquarians. They named your constellation Aquarius.

YOUR RULING PLANET: Wild and Weird Uranus

Uranus is the star of extremes and change. He is your *spirited born-free* planet. Uranus is definitely the rebellious oddball of the solar system. It is the only planet that lies on its side instead of standing straight up. Probably to get a totally different worldview, like yours! Its magnetic field is also different from every other planet's. It's not in the center, but tilted at 60 degrees. It goes through forty-two years of daylight and then forty-two years of darkness during its eighty-four year orbit around the Sun. It is all blue. Electric blue. Interesting again, because Uranus rules electricity. Electricity and all things that *shock*. Like sudden insights, flashes of intuition, inspiration, and yes, *you*, interesting Aquarian! It was discovered in 1781, when revolutions were *all* over the place. The American Revolution, the French Revolution, the Industrial Revolution—Uranus changes things, for sure!

WHO WAS YOUR URANUS?

Uranus was the ancient Greek sky god, and the first ruler of the universe. He was gifted with foresight and great vision. Having Uranus as your guiding star means you, too, have this gift.

THE PARTS OF YOUR BODY THAT AQUARIUS RULES:
Your Circulation, Ankles, and Shins

Your ankles and shins must still be reverberating from the Great Flood! They are extra-sensitive, so be careful wearing high heels. And your blood must have almost frozen in the water . . . you are prone to chills, even now.

IN YOUR ELEMENT: Air

Some people think you are a water sign, but you're not. The water link is from your original title of water pourer. It describes the way you pour ideas and inspiration into the world. You are an air sign, like Gemini and Libra. Air means "thinking," which you do all the time!

YOUR LUCKY . . .

☆ **Colors:** Your lucky colors are freezing electric neon blue and yellow-orange. The colors of electricity!

☆ **Metal:** Uranium. Aquarius-style, this is not even really a metal. It is a metallic, radioactive chemical, existing solely in combinations. It endures continuous fission!

☆ **Precious stone:** Amethyst

☆ **Day of the week:** Wednesday. It is the fastest day because it is speedy Mercury's day. So, schedule what you want to go extra-fast on Wednesdays.

IN SCHOOL

You're so quick at getting stuff, you can fly right over the rules of *how* to get it. You're more interested in your own way. You stare out the window a lot, even though you might be the brightest student. Your classmates count on you to say something different!

WITH YOUR TEACHERS

They are puzzled when you can answer the hardest question right, but forget a simple spelling. Still, they treat you with respect. They recognize a kid with natural smarts when they see one.

ON THE PLAYGROUND

You go back and forth between hanging out with your million friends and being alone. You can't stand being bored. Are you working on a new experiment yet?

WITH YOUR FRIENDS

You have friends of all types. You can have one best friend one week, then another one the next week. You are a great loyal friend to them all! You're also a master problem-solver.

WITH YOUR FAMILY

Before your family puts your picture on the side of a milk carton, try to spend more time with them! They embarrass you sometimes, but don't worry: You'll become super-attached to them when you're older.

TRUE LOVE

You thrill with the discovery of someone new, but if they zone in on your freedom, you fall out of love fast. You'll know your first love by its psychic bond. You won't ever forget it. **Best Love Matches:** Gemini, Libra, Aquarius, Sagittarius and, once in a while, Aries.

WHICH SIGNS YOU GROOVE WITH; Which Signs You Don't

The easiest signs are the other air signs, Gemini and Libra. They think as much as you do, so that's interesting. Sagittarius makes life more fun, and Aries is great as long as they're not giving orders. You hate that! You can take or leave Capricorn and Leo—who also like to give orders—but with Scorpio and Taurus you will want to bring out your famous Aquarian compassion. It will help you understand how a proud eagle (Scorpio) wants the world a certain way, and how a strong bull (Taurus) hates to give up their ground.

HOW TO SPOT AN AQUARIUS

I'm turning this over to George Bernard Shaw, who described "genius" the best. (Of course, he's a Leo!) He said: *"A genius is a person who, seeing farther and probing deeper than other people, has a different set of ethical valuations from theirs, and has energy enough to give effect to this extra vision and its valuations in whatever manner best suits his or her specific talents."* I know there are long words in there, but you're an Aquarian, so it won't be a problem! When you see some-one doing their own thing, going out on a limb (as Aquarian Julia Butterfly Hill did when climbing that tree!), or just staring off into space, that'll be an Aquarian. The Aquarian stare is focused, and they  might even squint their eyes in concentration. They don't blink. That's a dead giveaway to spotting an Aquarian, and you can just bet they're thinking of some new idea; something innovative and totally original!

Okay, So You're Not an Aquarius . . .

☆ **But Your Crush Is**

Say something fascinating! Brush up on being like a mystery. Your crush can't resist that. And forget about being jealous; Aquarians talk to everyone. **Secret Tip:** Your crush can sometimes turn cold, and all of a sudden, too—don't take it personally!

☆ **But Your Best Friend Is**

You learn something new from Aquarian best friends every day. They *never* bore you. The down side is, they disappear. One moment, they're there, the next, they're not. It's not magic. They just need alone time. Also, don't ask what they think of your new hairstyle if you're not prepared to hear the truth.

☆ **But Your Brand-new Friend Is**

You are excited by this brand-new friend. At the same time, your new pal manages to infuriate you in the first moments of your new friendship. He or she is always telling you something you don't want to hear!

☆ But Your Teacher Is

Aquarian teachers get you to think differently. They challenge you. There's always something different going on in an Aquarian's classroom. They're the best. But, man, are they tough on grading!

☆ But Your Parent Is

Aquarian parents are way cool, even though they sometimes forget to do the *basic* parent stuff. They tell you to stand up for yourself all the time. Sometimes they're *too* cool, as in not giving you enough hugs. But they pay ultraattention, and you know they'd do anything for you.

☆ But Your Sister or Brother Is

You wonder why your sibling makes such trouble with the 'rents. Aquarian kids are always saying no, or arguing for their kid rights. You like them, but you think they're kind of *weird*. You also think their friends are weird. But don't tell them that. If you criticize them, forget it.

☆ But Your Pet Is

Aquarius kitties look like they're from *Alice in Wonderland*. They've got huge dreamy eyes and are always seeing something invisible, and then chasing it like maniacs. Forget about training the dogs. They want you to be happy, though, so if you try a different approach, it might work!

AQUARIUS ASTRO-JOTTER

AQUARIUS STARLETS
Brandy: February 11, 1979
Nick Carter (Backstreet Boys): January 28, 1980
Christina Ricci: February 12, 1980
Mena Suvari: February 9, 1979
Justin Timberlake: January 31, 1981

AQUARIUS HIGHEST HONORS
Charles Darwin, formulated theory of evolution: February 12, 1809
Galileo, astronomer: February 15, 1564
Abraham Lincoln, president: February 12, 1809

FAVORITE AQUARIUS CHARACTERS
Harriet the Spy
Mickey Mouse
Snoopy (*Peanuts*)

PISCES

YOUR SPECIAL TIME: February 20–March 20

You are born *so* close to spring, to light and warmth, that you can almost taste it. No other sign is more tempted to daydream about the future. It is the very end of winter, the darkest, coldest time of the year. Pisces likes to be in a small place to feel warm and safe.

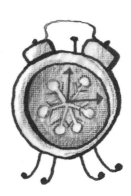

YOUR AWESOME TRAITS

You are the kindest sign of the zodiac. You love critters! And you wouldn't be caught dead saying no to a friend. You have great artistic vision and are always helping someone, somewhere. You are also sensitive, sympathetic, impressionable, imaginative, compassionate, forgiving, funny, tolerant, romantic, and a dreamer. Not surprisingly, Pisces rules poetry. Whatever their vocation, true Pisces will always create poems for the world. Pisces who have given "poems" to the world include: Albert Einstein, Sidney Poitier, Michelangelo, Copernicus, Dr. Seuss, and Jane Goodall. As Pisces Willy Wonka sang, *"There is no life I know that compares to pure imagination."* He was singing for imaginative Pisces everywhere.

OF ALL THE ANIMALS, YOU ARE MOST LIKE . . . *Two* Fish

Being a fish is very special! You swim in the watery depths of feeling and knowledge. The two fish swimming in two different directions spell out your choice in life: You can fight your way upstream, or float along at the bottom. You have so many gifts, you owe it to yourself to fight your way upstream!

WHO WAS YOUR PISCES?

Venus and Cupid were walking down the Euphrates River when the great and terrible monster Typhon suddenly appeared and flashed his hundred heads. "Oh, no!" cried Venus and Cupid. They froze in terror. They could not move, so Venus summoned her father Jupiter, god of all the gods. Jupiter arrived and changed them into two fishes. They jumped into the river and swam away. You are *still* like fairies who escape at the last minute!

YOUR RULING PLANET: Dreamy Hypnotic Neptune

Neptune is the star of dreams, the unconscious, and everything unseen. It is your psychic *X-Files* planet. It has a mysterious liquid core and many unseen moons. Your star is 2.7 billion miles away, can you imagine? If you could drive a car from

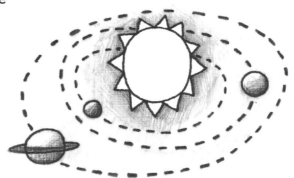

Neptune to the Sun, it would take you 4,400 years! Neptune has the strongest winds of any planet in the solar system—1,500 miles per hour. (Pisces, more than any other sign, can feel buffeted by life's winds!) Neptune was discovered in 1846, when hypnotism became a medical treatment, and anaesthetics were first used. Anaesthetics put us "out" into the unconscious, which Neptune rules. Freud was born, and so was psychology. This is Neptune!

WHO WAS YOUR NEPTUNE?

Called Poseidon by the Greeks, Neptune was king of all the watery depths. Like the dreamworld where all our secret thoughts and desires reside, water is dreamy and fluid, and

symbolizes imagination, emotion, and the unconscious. Neptune rules water, and inspires us all to swim upstream toward our greatest dreams.

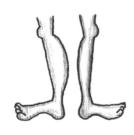

THE PART OF YOUR BODY THAT PISCES RULES: Your Feet

Believe it or not, you don't even *have* feet—you have fins! That's why it's so hard, but necessary, for Pisces to "keep their feet on the ground!" You get aches, corns, and bunions more than any other sign. So you must always make sure your shoes fit well!

IN YOUR ELEMENT: Water

Water is pure feeling and rules the unconscious and ESP. You are the only sign that exists purely in water. This is the world you live in!

"I love the water! I love swimming, I love diving —anything to do with water I love!"

—Kate, Pisces

YOUR LUCKY . . .

☆ **Colors:** Your lucky colors are turquoise and pale green. The underwater light of the sea.

☆ **Metal:** Platinum

☆ **Precious stone:** Aquamarine. It gives the gift of foresight.

☆ **Day of the week:** Friday. Venusians make your life easier, and Friday is Venus's day. So, schedule the things you want to go easily for Fridays. And they will!

IN SCHOOL

You seem to grasp subjects by pure ESP! But you need to develop discipline for subjects that don't interest you. You are so artistic and creative that you could be the top of your class in art, music, dance, or drama.

WITH YOUR TEACHERS

The best teachers for you are the ones who encourage your confidence and self-assurance. You look up to your teachers and like to idolize them. If you don't, you feel disappointed.

ON THE PLAYGROUND

You love to play make-believe. In your daydreams you're a major leaguer hitting a home run, or a princess discovering gold, or an inventor who's just discovered the cure for war. Whatever your fantasy, you're busy doing something fantastic.

WITH YOUR FRIENDS

You are the angel who always helps friends in need. You have fun with your friends and like to hang out with one or two special ones. It's to your benefit to be extra-choosy. Your moods and sense of balance are very influenced by who you're around.

WITH YOUR FAMILY

You're the sensitive one in your family (unless there's another Pisces!). You love to be made a fuss of, but you like your privacy, too. Arguments are *not* your scene. You can avoid them by explaining yourself clearly.

TRUE LOVE

You dream about the ideal love. It's like a quest for you. But sometimes you feel so shy! Your perfect match will understand you and never take your generous nature for granted.
Best Love Matches: Cancer, Scorpio, Taurus, Virgo, and Pisces

WHICH SIGNS YOU GROOVE WITH; Which Signs You Don't

The easiest signs are other water signs. You guys understand one another

without talking. Earth signs make your next best friends. Air signs can come and go too much. Fire signs can be loud and overwhelming. But, really, Pisces you're a friend to the world. You groove with just about everyone. Sometimes it would be better for you if you didn't!

HOW TO SPOT A PISCES

You can always tell a Pisces by their *eyes*. Always. Pisces eyes are full of feeling. They look like they're about to cry. Not in a bad way. They just look soulful and teary. It's incredible, but true! You know how Freddie Prinze, Jr.'s eyes look? And how Billy

Zane always looks like he has eye makeup on? Go look at them right now. They are perfect Pisces models. Take a look also at the Pisces eyes of Chris Klein, Jennifer Love Hewitt, and Shaquille O'Neal—see what I mean? It's something special about the eyes. Pisces Elizabeth Taylor has the most famous eyes in history—they are true violet. This Pisces eye-trait may be because the eye is the only body part that shows liquid on its surface, and Pisces is the only sign that is *all* water. Whatever the reason, the eyes are a giveaway. Try it! You won't be disappointed.

OKAY, SO YOU'RE NOT A PISCES . . .

☆ But Your Crush Is

Pisces won't show their feelings until they know how *you* feel. Their coolness and distance is only an act of self-protection. They are gentle souls who need to be treated with kid gloves. ***Secret Tip:*** If you go out, you may have to pick up the tab! Pisces are notorious for this.

☆ But Your Best Friend Is

Best friends who are Pisces are the sweetest in the world. It's fun to explore with them, and talk about one another's greatest dreams. Oh, but when they get sad (which happens quite a lot), you wish they would lighten up on the self-pity! Otherwise, it's like quicksand pulling you down.

☆ But Your Brand-new Friend Is

Your brand-new friend is intriguing and funny. Your pal makes cute jokes and funny sounds, and his or her sarcasm about certain people is hysterical! It's fun being led into Wonderland by a bona fide elf.

☆ But Your Teacher Is

The whole class thinks their Pisces teacher is really nice. They know he or she cares about them. Grooving with their students is easy, but the teaching part is harder because Pisces have a hard time looking outside themselves. They'll teach the way they understand it, but not necessarily the way you guys do! Just explain.

☆ But Your Parent Is

Your Pisces parent is not exactly what we'd call a big discipliner. Your mom or dad is great for playing with, for telling stories, and for cuddling, and if you need a good cry. He or she is very gentle and doesn't like to fight. Pisces 'rents offer to do *everything* for their kids. But sometimes you want to be the grown-up and take care of *them*.

☆ But Your Sister or Brother Is

You can joke and laugh with Pisces siblings nonstop. But when they retreat into their room or wherever they go, it's like they disappear. You can't make them come out. You wish your parents were millionaires, because one thing you can already tell about your Pisces sibling is this: When he or she grows up, your sib won't want to get an ordinary job and make money. Pisces think they can live off fairy dust if they have to.

☆ But Your Pet Is

One day my Pisces cat showed me a deep truth about Pisces. I was standing in the kitchen and Juno was sitting in the sink, grinning at me. (She grins, unlike other cats.) It was like we were in our own little world. Suddenly, a loud banging noise started from outside. She looked at me accusingly, eyes wide, like *what are you doing?* And terrified, she darted away. She thought *I'd* made the loud banging noise! She'd been so in "our moment" that she couldn't fathom that the disturbance was from anywhere else. She showed me the imagination of Pisces pets, and how deeply they live in their own world.

PISCES ASTRO-JOTTER

PISCES STARLETS
Jamie Bell: March 14, 1986
Thora Birch: March 11, 1982
Charlotte Church: February 21, 1986
Taylor Hanson: March 14, 1983
Jake Lloyd: March 3, 1989

PISCES HIGHEST HONORS
Albert Einstein, scientist: March 14, 1879
Jane Goodall, chimpanzee expert: March 4, 1934
Dr. Seuss, children's book author: March 2, 1904

FAVORITE PISCES CHARACTERS
Bambi
Cindy Brady (*The Brady Bunch*)
Willy Wonka (*Charlie and the Chocolate Factory*)